1979-1998

Garlic Lovers'

GREATEST HITS

20

YEARS *of* PRIZE-WINNING RECIPES

CELESTIAL ARTS
BERKELEY, CALIFORNIA

Distributed in Canada by Ten Speed Canada, in the United Kingdom and
Europe by Airlift Books, in New Zealand by Tandem Press, in Australia
by Simon & Schuster Australia, in Singapore and Malaysia by Berkeley
Books, and in South Africa by Real Books.

Photographs by Bill Strange and Tommy Gibson
Cover design by Shelley Firth
Cover photograph by John Gavrilis
Text design by Ken Scott
Illustrations by Bill Nelson and Shirley Wong
Typesetting by Star Type and Shelley Firth
Cover logo trademarked and copyrighted 1979 by the Gilroy Garlic
Festival Association, Inc.

FIRST CELESTIAL ARTS PRINTING 1993

Library of Congress Cataloging-in-Publication Data

Garlic lover's greatest hits: 20 years of prize-winning recipes.
    p. cm.
  Recipes from the Gilroy Garlic Festival, Gilroy, California
  ISBN 0-89087-698-3
  1. Cookery (Garlic). I. Gilroy Garlic Festival.
TX819.G375 1993
641.6'526—dc20   93-20613
                                                           CIP

  2 3 4 5 / 02 01 00 99 98

DEDICATION

To the people of Gilroy for sharing a lifestyle of good food, good times and for giving from the heart.

THE BEGINNING

Memories by Rudy Melone

*O*nce the decision was made, it took only three months to put the first annual Gilroy Garlic Festival together.

Well actually, it really wasn't all that simple and there was only a handful of us that believed it was worth a try. We had our skeptics, including the Rotary Club and the Chamber of Commerce, neither of which was willing to take the plunge and sponsor the event. With $200 from Bert Mantelli the Gilroy Garlic Festival Association was made legal by the State of California in June, 1979, and we were off and running.

The event was staged at the Bloomfield Ranch just south of Gilroy, adjacent to Don Christopher's garlic field. The garlic had just been harvested, and the field became our parking lot. The ranch had a very large house, with a big front yard and a smaller back yard. It was in the back that we set up the first Gourmet Alley, with Val Filice and a group of his farmers/chefs who prepared garlic-laden foods for Festival guests. There were a few other booths by private vendors, and a small concrete stage that was used for entertainment. The front included a few vendors, another entertainment stage, the beer concession run by the Chamber of Commerce, and a Pepsi booth run by the Gilroy Rotary Club. Bob Dyer and I emceed at the two different stages.

Though we had financial backing thanks to loans from Christopher Ranch, Gilroy Foods, Nob Hill Foods, and Goldsmith Seeds, we were still concerned about paying for the costs of the event. So we staged a barn dance at Christopher Ranch the week before, and even hosted a breakfast on the first morning of the festival to try to raise extra coin.

A nervous group of garlic-loving risk-takers who fussed with the last minute preparations on Saturday, August 3, 1979 (the first day of the two-day event) knew they had a winner when two things happened: we ran out of tickets and had to re-sell those that were collected at the gate, and when the first Festival-goers gasped with delight as the calamari, dropped from Val Filice's hand, flamed up from the huge frying pan.

But, there was more to the Festival than the events on the Bloomfield grounds. They included a 10K run, a golf tournament, a recipe and cook-off contest, tours of garlic-related industries, and a beauty pageant to crown the Miss Gilroy Garlic Festival Queen. They all went off without a hitch. There was only one miscue — an Elvis Presley look/sound-alike show that had technical problems.

The best estimate of attendance that first year was between 22,000 and 25,000. We lost count of everything else because it all happened so fast — pounds of garlic used, pounds of calamari, shrimp, vegetables, etc., all had to be ordered and re-ordered to meet the unexpectedly large turnout.

I conceived of the Gilroy Garlic Festival primarily to promote the community of Gilroy and to enhance its image, its garlic industry specifically and its agri-business in general. In seeking to enhance the image of Gilroy, the original Festival Board of Directors designated that any surplus funds would be used, first, to guarantee the continuation of the Festival; second, to assist the Gilroy Chamber of Commerce to become self-sufficient in its efforts to serve the community of Gilroy; and finally, to assist the charities and non-profit organizations of the area through compensation for the work of their volunteers.

The first Garlic Festival and the succeeding Festivals have truly helped to achieve those goals. I wish I could thank those persons who provided special help and entertainment during the first event. Space does not permit. However, a special note of appreciation should go to those pioneers who believed in the event and did yeoman work in making the first Festival happen. They are listed below with their activity.

This book of recipes is a special reflection of the success of the Garlic Festival and the widespread devotion of hundreds of thousands of people to the bountiful bulb of garlic. Enjoy it in the best of health. Salud!

The annual Gilroy Garlic Festival has grown from a small food editors' luncheon into one of America's largest urban fairs.
FAMILY WEEKLY

1979 BOARD OF DIRECTORS AND COMMITTEE CHAIRS

Board of Directors
Dr. Rudy Melone - President
Mr. Don Christopher - Vice President
Mr. Joseph Filice - Treasurer
Mr. Hy Miller
Ms. Lynda Trelut
Ms. Reenel Moretti - Financial Secretary

Arts & Crafts
Barn Dance - Norie Goforth, Chairman; Ron Mingus, Co-Chair
Beauty Pageant - Gina Read, Chairman
Booths - Forrest Barriger, Chairman
Entertainment - Judy Latronica, Chairman
Finance - Joe Filice, Chairman
Golf Tournament - Robert Infelise, Chairman
Gourmet Alley - Tim Filice, Chairman; Fred Domino, Co-Chair

Hospitality
Logistics - Bill Ayer, Chairman
Parking - Carl Swank, Chairman
Printed Program - Carol Dyer, Chairman
Promotion - Bob Dyer, Chairman; Karen Christopher, Co-Chair
Recipe Contest - Rose Emma Pelliccione, Chairman
Tickets - Fred Wood, Chairman
Tours - Ken Vantress, Chairman
10 K Run - Bill Flodberg, Chairman

©1979 G.G.F.A. Inc.

v

CONTENTS

PEPPER STEAK SANDWICH
and PASTA CON PESTO

PEPPER STEAK FACTS
WE USE: FINEST MID-WEST BEEF

15,800 LBS.	TOP SIRLOIN
1,500 GAL.	BELL PEPPERS
750 GAL.	ONIONS
1,500 GAL.	CHOPPED GARLIC
200 LBS.	BUTTER
6,000 LBS.	CHARCOAL

OUR BASTE Lemon Juice, White Wine, Olive Oil, Salt & Pepper, Oregano, Chopped Garlic, Rosemary Brush.

DIAMOND SIGNS (408) 947-8601

PASTA CON PESTO
WE USE:

6,000 LBS.	PASTA
175 GAL.	PESTO
75 GAL.	CHOPPED G
800 LBS.	BUTTER
50 GAL.	OLIVE OIL
20 CASES	PARMESAN

Our appx. 300 Volunteers work over 4000 H

★ ALL PROCEEDS PRESENTED TO THE GILROY GOES DIRECTLY TO CHARITABLE CAUSES.

THE GILROY GARLIC FESTIVAL

*W*ether you appreciate garlic for its flavor, its health aspects, or its folklore, you'll want to travel to Gilroy and experience the annual Garlic Festival. Seeing is believing!

The ultimate in summer food fairs, the Garlic Festival features a truly intemational array of epicurean garlic delights. Gourmet Alley is the heart of this food showcase, where local chefs perform culinary magic over the firepits in full view of spectators. These wizards work wonders with iron skillets the size of bicycle wheels as they toss the flaming calamari or gently saute bright red and green peppers to add to the top sirloin in Pepper Beefsteak Sandwiches. Mouthwatering mountains of garlic bread, tons of scamp) swimming in lobster butter sauce, delicate Stuffed Mushrooms, and cauldrons of Pasta Con Pesto all set the high standards for quality and adherence to the garlic theme that prevails throughout the Festival.

Eighty additional food booths operated by senice clubs, civic and merchant groups offer a breathtaking variety of garlic creations. After sampling the aromatic offerings of the talented townspeople of Gilroy, visitors can cool their palates with the local wines, a cool drink, or garlic ice cream and desserts of local fresh fruits.

Thousands of garlic garlands and braids and the mouthwatering aromas from the outdoor kitchens create the perfect setting for the garlic displays and demonstrations. Merchandise and exhibit booths offer an array of garlicthemed articles such as fresh garlic (pee-wees to colossal), garlic braids, wreaths, lets, dry decorative arrangements, all forms of dehydrated and processed garlic levee deodorized), garlic pills, cookbooks, and information on garlic uses and its health aspects, folklore, garlic hats, tee shirts, jewelry... just let your imagination go! It will probably be there.

And then there is "Art Alley, " one hundred booths of juried fine arts and crafts featuring many original works pertaining to the theme of garlic. Musicians and theatrical groups perform continuously throughout each day of the Festival with the emphasis on family entertainment.

Miss Gilroy Garlic Festival will reign and Festival goers will be encouraged to participate in the garlic braiding and the garlic "topping" {a garlic harvesting technique which removes the tops and roots with sharp shears) and to obsene the Great Garlic Recipe Cook-off, described in the next section.

Add to these ingredients a generous dash of Califomia small town conviviality, and the result is a recipe for a truly unique summer experience whose savory memories will be with you long after the participants take their garlic braids, cookbooks, and totes full of garliciana home.

*P*eople flocked to this little farming community 80 miles south of San Francisco. When the crowds weren't eating, they were singing garlic songs, swapping garlic seeds and recipes ...buying garlic souvernirs

CHRISTIAN SCIENCE MONITOR

xi

THE GILROY GARLIC FESTIVAL RECIPE CONTEST

*F*rom the beginning, the Garlic Recipe Contest held each year in connection with the Gilroy Garlic Festival was intended to be first and foremost a wonderful adventure in garlic cookery rather than a commercial enterprise. Because the Festival's primary purpose is to support local charities, it was decided to keep the prizes relatively small so that more of the proceeds from the festival could be contributed to charitable organizations. Top prize is $1000. In addition, the entrants who qualify each year for the final cook-off, held during the festival, are expected to bring their own pots, pans and ingredients.

Nearly 1000 entries pour in every year from garlic lovers throughout the United States who want to share their great garlic cooking discoveries with others who would truly appreciate them.

Contest rules specify that recipes must call for 6 cloves of fresh garlic or the equivalent in dehydrated or processed garlic. Recipes must be original, and only amateur chefs are permitted to enter the contest. When recipes are received at the Festival office, the volunteer committee chairman and committee members sort through the recipes eliminating those which do not meet the specific rules of the contest.

The top 100 qualifying recipes are then sent to a food consultant who is in the business of developing new recipes for food clients and who understand all the problems related to such endeavors. She carefully reads and compares recipes, searching for the unusual technique or combination of ingredients that might make a particular recipe a winner. If there are any questions about a recipe it is prepared exactly as specified by the entrant and then taste-tested to ensure that it qualifies to be in the finals. Once the prejudging is done, the finalists are not)fied to be sure that they will be able to participate in the cook-off where the winners will be selected.

Judges who serve at the cook-off are chosen from the professional food world for their knowledge and personal food expertise. Many have judged the most important cooking contests in the country yet all agree that the Garlic Recipe Contest is the most fun.

All recipes entered in the contest become the property of the Gilroy Garlic Festival Association.

Request rules from or send recipes to:
GILROY GARLIC FESTIVAL
P.O. Box 2311
Gilroy, California 95021

*G*arlic laced specialities were prepared in gigantic pans from morning to night as wave after wave of festival goers followed their noses to the bustling outdoor kitchen area.

VACAVILLE *REPORTER*

GILROY, CALIFORNIA is a town of

35,000 located in the fertile Santa Clara Valley, 80 miles south of San Francisco. Its livelihood is derived from a variety of agricultural products, among which is an especially important crop. It is estimated that garlic is a $65 million industry in Gilroy and within a 90-mile radius, 90 percent of the garlic grown and processed in the United States can be found. Gilroy is also the home of two of the major dehydration plants and three of the major fresh garlic shippers in the world. An estimated 100 million pounds of garlic is grown, processed, or distributed through Gilroy each year. With all this in its favor and the desire to stage an unparalleled celebration that would attract garlic lovers nationally and internationally, Gilroy claimed the title of Garlic Capital of the World during the first annual festival in 1979.

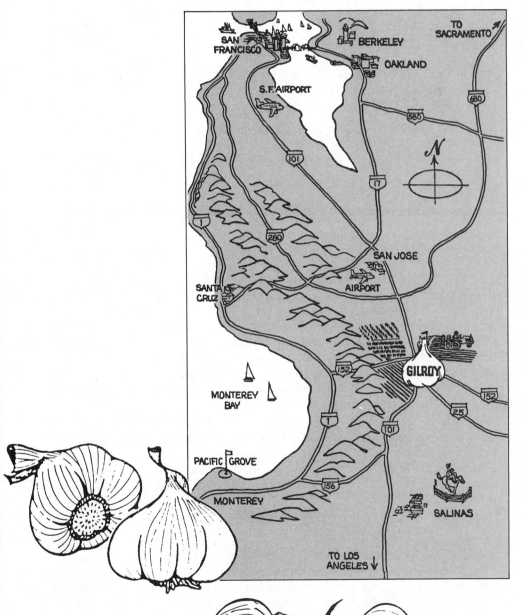

Driving north from San Juan Bautista you can usually count on abundant advance warning that you are approaching Gilroy. When the wind is blowing the right way, the unmistaken aroma of garlic can be detected in the air for many miles around.

MICHAEL DORMAN

GOOD THINGS TO KNOW ABOUT GARLIC

KNOW YOUR GARLIC

Fresh garlic may be creamy white or have a purplish-red cast, but whatever the color, it should be plump and firm, with its paperlike covering intact, not spongy, soft, or shriveled.

Dehydrated or other forms of processed garlic should be purchased in tightly sealed containers, preferably from markets where there is sufficient traffic to ensure that the spices are fresh.

HOW BEST TO STORE

Fresh garlic keeps best in a cool, dry place with plenty of ventilation. It should not be refrigerated unless you separate the cloves and immerse them in oil, either peeled or unpeeled. If the garlic isn't peeled, the cloves will hold their firmness longer, but peeling will be more difficult. Fresh garlic which is held in open-air storage for any length of time will lose some of its pungency and may even develop sprouts. The garlic is still usable, but will be somewhat milder and more will be needed to achieve the same strength of flavor in a dish being prepared.

Dehydrated forms of garlic should be stored with other spices in as cool and dry a place as possible, definitely not above or next to the kitchen range or sink or in front of a window with exposure to the sun. Keep tightly sealed. Processed garlic which requires refrigeration after opening should, of course, always be stored in the refrigerator to maintain its quality.

HOW TO PEEL

If you are peeling only a few cloves, simply press each clove against the cutting board with the flat side of a heavy kitchen knife or press between the thumb and forefinger to loosen the skin first. If your recipe calls for a larger quantity of garlic, drop the cloves in boiling water for just a minute and drain quickly. They will peel quite easily. If you have a microwave oven, you can cook the cloves for 5 seconds or so to achieve the same effect.

MUST GARLIC BE PEELED?

Not necessarily. You can cook unpeeled garlic in a hot pan—it won't burn easily—then slip off the skins when the garlic is soft. Or, if the garlic is cooked in a soup or sauce and then the whole cloves discarded, there is certainly no necessity to peel them. And, if you are preparing a dish such as "Forty Clove Chicken," cook the cloves unpeeled and then simply press the soft garlic out of the skin with your fingers or with knife and fork as you eat them.

WHICH TO USE

Whether you use fresh, dehydrated, or processed garlic is a matter of personal choice. Fresh garlic fans note that garlic flavors food differently, depending on how it is used. Fresh uncooked garlic is most pungent when pureed, crushed, or finely minced. For milder garlic flavor, keep cloves whole or cut in large pieces. Whole cloves cooked for a long time with roasts, stews, or soups have a surprisingly sweet, nut-like flavor. It is very important when cooking with fresh garlic not to burn it. When garlic is burned, it has a very bitter flavor and must discarded or it will ruin the flavor of the dish. Remember, when sautéing garlic in oil, keep the heat fairly low and cook it until it is just very lightly browned.

Other forms of garlic vary somewhat in their flavoring characteristics, but you can generally plan on the following substitutions:

1 average-size clove = ⅛ teaspoon dehydrated, powdered, minced,
    of fresh garlic   or chopped garlic

or

½ teaspoon garlic salt. (*Caution:* when using garlic salt in recipes calling for fresh garlic, decrease the amount of salt called for.)

GARLIC ODOR

Several techniques help to control the odor of garlic on the hands that results from peeling or chopping. Disposable plastic gloves can be worn while performing this chore. Or you can rub the fingers with salt and lemon juice afterwards, then rinse under cold water. The best solution we have found is to rub the fingers under the bowl of a stainless steel teaspoon under running water for a few moments. There is a chemical reaction which takes place that does indeed eliminate the odor from the fingers. The more garlic chopped, the longer it will take to remove the odor, but it can be done! Garlic odor on the breath is most easily controlled by eating fresh parsley. Parsley has been called "nature's mouthwash" by garlic lovers because of its effectiveness. Chewing on a coffee bean or two also seems to do the trick.

There's no such thing as a little garlic.
SAN DIEGO *UNION*

TO CHOP OR PRESS?

There are some who swear by their garlic press and others who claim that using a garlic press makes the fresh garlic taste bitter. It is certainly a quick and easy method of mincing garlic; however, you do lose some of the pulp which means that hand-chopped gives a better yield and less waste. Again, the choice is yours. If you choose to chop the garlic by hand, here's a tip from the wife of a garlic grower: Add the salt required for your recipe directly into the minced garlic while it is still on the cutting board. The salt will absorb the juices and make it easier to scoop the tiny garlic pieces off the board.

GARLIC FLAVORED OIL, VINEGAR, OR SALT

It's easy to flavor with garlic by adding peeled whole cloves of garlic to bottles of oil or vinegar for two or three days before using. To make garlic salt, just bury 3 peeled and pressed garlic cloves in half a cup of salt. Add fresh ground pepper and ground ginger to taste, if you like. Let stand for a few days in a screw-top jar. Remove garlic and use the salt as desired to flavor soups, meats, salads, etc.

GARLIC BUTTER

Make logs of garlic butter and freeze them to have on hand to melt on broiled meats or mix into fresh cooked vegetables or spread on bread. Just add mashed garlic cloves or the equivalent in dehydrated or processed garlic to suit your taste to sticks of butter (about 6 cloves fresh garlic per stick is recommended). If you wish, add a few herbs and salt lightly. Form into logs, wrap in plastic and freeze. Slice off as needed.

BAKED WHOLE HEADS

One of the most popular ways to serve fresh garlic is to bake whole heads to serve as an hors d'oeuvre with crunchy bread or as an accompaniment to meat or vegetables. Peel as much of the outer skin away as possible, leaving the cloves unpeeled and the head intact. Place heads in covered casserole or on a piece of heavy aluminum foil, drizzle with olive oil, dot with butter, salt and pepper to taste, and bake covered at 350 degrees for about 45 minutes or until cloves are soft and can be squeezed easily out of their skins onto bread or other foods.

TERMS

Clove. One of the several segments of a bulb, each of which is covered with a thin, papery skin.

Crushed. A term which refers to fresh garlic which has been smashed by the broad side of a knife or cleaver on a chopping board or with a rolling pin between several thicknesses of waxed paper.

Dehydrated. Any of several forms of garlic from which the moisture has been removed. Dehydrated garlic is available minced, powdered, and granulated.

Fresh. The term used to describe garlic which has not been dehydrated. Actually "fresh" garlic is allowed to "cure" in the field before harvesting just until the papery skin, not the cloves, becomes dry.

Garlic Braid. A garland of fresh garlic braided together by its tops. Braiding is done while the garlic is still only partially cured with some moisture remaining in the tops and before the tops are removed in harvesting. When they become fully dried, they are too brittle to braid. Originally devised as a convenient storage method, garlic braids are quite decorative and have become popular in this country as a kitchen adornment. Serious garlic lovers like to use them for cooking purposes, cutting off one bulb at a time from the braid. Care should be taken if the braid is to be preserved as a decoration that it is not handled carelessly. The papery covering of the bulb is fragile and will break easily when the garlic itself has shriveled after a year or so.

Granulated. A dehydrated form of garlic that is five times stronger than raw garlic. Its flavor is released only in the presence of moisture.

Juice. Garlic juice may be purchased commercially or prepared by squeezing fresh cloves in a garlic press, being certain not to include any of the flesh. Juice blends easily for uniform flavor.

Minced. This term is used for both dehydrated and fresh garlic. Generally called for when small pieces of garlic are desirable as in soups, sauces, or salad dressings. Fresh garlic may be minced using a sharp knife on a chopping board. If the recipe calls for salt, add it to the garlic while mincing. It will prevent the garlic from sticking to the knife and absorb the juices otherwise lost in the mincing process. Finely minced garlic, as called for in most French recipes, tends to disappear into the finished dish. For a more robust flavor, mince more coarsely, as called for in many Chinese dishes. Large amounts of garlic can be minced using a blender or food processor.

Powdered. Powdered garlic is available commercially. When using powder in recipes with a high acid content, mix with water (two parts water to one part powder) before adding. Powdered garlic can be made from fresh by slowly drying peeled garlic cloves in the oven. When very dry, pound or crush until fine and powdery. Pass through a sieve and pound.

Pressed. A term for garlic which has been put through a garlic press. There are many different types of presses available, some even "self-cleaning." When using a garlic press, it isn't necessary to peel the garlic clove. Simply cut it in half and place in the press. Then squeeze. The skin will stay behind, making the press easier to clean. Remember to clean your press immediately after use before the small particles which remain behind have a chance to dry.

Puree. A term for garlic which has been cooked at high heat and then pressed through a sieve. Available commercially or made at home. It is excellent to have on hand to blend into soups, sauces, or to spread on slices of bread to serve with hors d'oeuvres.

Garlic Salt. Available commercially, it is usually a blend of approximately 90% salt, approximately 9% garlic, and approximately 1% free-flowing agent. When using garlic salt in recipes calling for fresh garlic, decrease the amount of salt called for.

RECOMMENDED PROPORTIONS

As cooks become more confident in the use of garlic and discover what wonders its flavor can perform with simple meat and vegetable dishes, they tend to use larger and larger quantities. For the beginner, who may be uncertain about how much garlic to use when experimenting with familiar recipes, we offer the following proportions of fresh or dehydrated garlic. Keep in mind that these are on the low side and most who really enjoy the flavor of garlic will want to use a great deal more.

Meats: For each 2 pounds of pork, beef, lamb or other meats, use ⅛ to ¼ teaspoon garlic powder, or 1½ to 2 teaspoons garlic salt, or 2 to 3 cloves fresh garlic.

Sauces: For 3 cups barbecue, tomato, or other sauce, use ⅛ to ¼ teaspoon garlic powder, or 2 to 3 cloves fresh garlic.

Soups: To 3 cups meat stock or vegetable soup, add ⅛ teaspoon garlic powder, or 2 cloves fresh garlic.

Pickled foods: Per quart of kosher-style dill pickles or per pint of dilled green beans, add ⅛ to ¼ teaspoon dehydrated chopped or minced garlic, or 2 to 3 cloves fresh garlic.

Relishes: To 2 pints of chutney or relish, add ⅛ teaspoon dehydrated minced garlic, or 2 cloves fresh garlic.

When was the last time you saw a vampire in Gilroy?

D.H.

1979

*The festival, which celebrates
the end of this year's garlic harvest,
really is smalltown Americana at its best.*

KEITH MUROAKA
THE (SANTA CRUZ) SENTINEL

GARLIC MUSHROOMS MORGAN HILL

LINDA TARVIN, Morgan Hill, CA

Linda was among the top ten finalists in the first Great Garlic Recipe Contest and her mushroom recipe drew raves not only for its flavor but for its attractive presentation with whole garlic bulbs used for decoration.

4	cloves fresh garlic, minced
1/3	cup olive oil
2/3	cup white wine vinegar
1/3	cup dry red *or* white wine
2	tablespoons soy sauce
2	tablespoons honey
2	tablespoons chopped parsley
1	tablespoon salt
2	lbs. fresh mushrooms

Sauté garlic in oil. Add vinegar, wine, soy sauce, honey, parsley and salt. Stir until mixture is well blended and hot.

Place mushrooms in heatproof container with tightly fitting lid. Pour hot mixture over mushrooms; allow to marinate from 1 to 3 hours, or more, turning over several times.

Save marinade for later use on more mushrooms or use it as a salad dressing.

Serves 4–6.

ANTIPASTO AGLIO

M. J. FILLICE, Gilroy, CA

This wonderful and imaginative appetizer is the creation of one of Gilroy's finest amateur chefs who devised it for his companions on a hunting trip. When prepared this way, garlic's assertive flavor is diminished to a delicate, nutlike taste. The recipe was selected as a finalist in the first Great Garlic Recipe Contest.

GARLIC ANTIPASTO:

Peel garlic cloves and slice centers 1/8 inch thick. Press ends through garlic press to yield 1/4 teaspoon.

Place pressed garlic in small bowl with anchovies. Add parsley, butter, 1 teaspoon oil, and Tabasco; mash to a paste. Cover and refrigerate.

Heat 1/4 cup oil, add garlic slices and sauté to a light golden brown—almost to a potato chip fry. *Do not overfry!*

Spread anchovy paste on toast. Garnish with garlic slices and WHAM-O!—the taste of tastes! Follow with a sip of robust red wine. *Salute e buon appetito!!*

Serves 6–8.

30	large cloves fresh garlic
1	can (2 oz.) anchovy fillets
1	tablespoon finely chopped parsley
1	tablespoon butter, melted
1	tablespoon olive oil Dash Tabasco
1/4	cup olive oil
	baguettes, 2 or 3 dozen thinly sliced and toasted pieces.

1

KELLY'S ASIAN CHICKEN

KELLY GREENE, Mill Valley, CA

This absolutely mouth-watering chicken dish was unanimously selected as the First Place Winner in the first Great Garlic Recipe Contest and Cook-off. It's a simple, inspired combination that takes only 20 minutes to put together. Serve with cooked Chinese noodles and then stand back and let the compliments fly!

1	3-½ lb. frying chicken, cut into serving pieces *or* the equivalent in chicken parts of your choice
3	tablespoons peanut oil
1	head (not clove) fresh garlic, peeled and coarsely chopped
2	small dried hot red peppers (optional)
¾	cup distilled white vinegar
¼	cup soy sauce
3	tablespoons honey

Heat oil in large, *heavy* skillet and brown chicken well on all sides, adding garlic and peppers toward the end.

Add remaining ingredients and cook over medium-high heat until chicken is done and sauce has been reduced somewhat. This will not take long, less than 10 minutes.

If you are cooking both white and dark meat, remove white meat first, so it does not dry out. Watch very carefully so that the sauce does not burn or boil away. There should be a quantity of sauce left to serve with the chicken, and the chicken should appear slightly glazed.

Serve with Chinese noodles, pasta, or rice.

Serves 4–6.

MOUTH-WATERING BAKED FISH

JEANNE MARKS, Aptos, CA

Jeanne Marks says of her truly mouth-watering baked fish, "The aroma knocks you out." Whole fish are not easy to come by and it's the fortunate chef whose good luck brings him a freshly caught salmon, bass, or snapper so he can enjoy this nearly effortless method for cooking it.

Rinse and dry fish and put into baking dish that has been sprayed with a nonstick spray. Combine all ingredients and pour over fish. Let stand at least 1 hour.

Bake in 400-degree oven for about 30 minutes or until fish flakes and has lost its transparency. Baste at least once during baking process.

Decorate top with lemon slices and paprika.

Serves 6–8.

8	to 10 lb. whole fish (salmon, sea bass, red snapper, etc.)
	Nonstick vegetable spray coating
¼	cup brandy *or* apple juice
½	cup onion flakes
¼	cup oil *or* melted butter
¼	cup lemon juice
¼	cup soy sauce
4	cloves fresh garlic, minced *or* pressed
2	tablespoons Worcestershire sauce
	Salt and pepper to taste
	Lemon slices
	Paprika

2

VEAL SHANKS WITH GARLIC

ANN EPSTEIN, North Hollywood, CA

*Ann Epstein, third place winner in the first Great Garlic Recipe Contest and Cook-off
cooked with four whole heads of garlic in her recipe for veal shanks.
Garlic and veal cook together in a wine sauce for about an hour or so and when ready,
the garlic is gathered in a dish and offered to guests to spread,
like butter, on toasted bread to eat with the meat.
Be sure to select a robust red wine to go with it.*

3	hind leg veal shanks, each cut into 3 or 4 1-inch pieces
½	cup oil (corn, peanut, soy, sesame, olive *or* a mixture)
3	large onions, thickly sliced
1	or 2 large carrots, thickly sliced
	Bouquet garni
1	cup dry white wine
2	to 3 cups brown veal stock *or* beef *or* chicken broth, enough to cover the meat
	Salt and pepper to taste
4	heads fresh garlic
	Fresh chopped parsley
	Bread, cut in thick slices and toasted

In a large braising pot, brown veal shanks in hot oil until golden on all sides. Remove meat.

Into hot oil, add onions, carrots, bouquet garni and toss until soft and golden brown. Spoon off as much fat as possible.

In the same pot, arrange cooked vegetables, then veal shanks, then wine. Reduce wine completely, taking care not to burn meat and vegetables.

Add the veal stock or meat broth. Bring to a boil.

Have ready all the cloves from the 4 heads of garlic—separated, peeled and mashed with a knife or mallet. Add these to simmering meat. Add salt and pepper.

Cover with a layer of foil, the sides of which have been turned up so that the steam will not dilute the sauce. Cover with pot lid. Bake in 325-degree oven for 1 to 1½ hours. Meat will be done when it pulls easily away from the bones.

There should be between 1½ to 2 cups of rich, thick sauce left. If more, reduce till required amount is reached. Onions and carrots can be left in the sauce as is; removed, pureed and added back; or removed entirely.

Place meat on a pretty platter. Sprinkle with parsley. Gather all mashed garlic cloves and place in a dish.

Serve meat and toasted slices of bread spread with mashed garlic. Because of the lengthy cooking, the garlic loses much of its pungency and becomes very rich and buttery in texture.

Makes 4 servings.

3

HOLLISTER VEGETABLE CASSEROLE

LENA LICO, Hollister, CA

A finalist in the Great Garlic Recipe Contest and Cook-off, Lena says this entry is a favorite with her family and some of the Gavilan College staff where she is manager of the cafeteria. "This dish is particularly good for vegetarians," says Lena. It would also be a good choice as a side dish to serve with barbecued meats.

6	zucchini, sliced
6	potatoes, peeled and sliced
3	bell peppers, cut in strips
2	large onions, sliced
1	large eggplant, sliced
½	cup Romano *or* Parmesan cheese
	Salt and pepper to taste
5	cloves fresh garlic, pressed
1	teaspoon oregano
8	large tomatoes, sliced *or* 2 lbs. canned tomatoes, broken up
½	cup oil

Place layers of vegetables in greased baking pan alternating with 4 tablespoons grated cheese, salt and pepper.

Combine garlic and oregano with tomatoes. Top the casserole with tomatoes and 4 tablespoons cheese. Drizzle oil over top.

Cover and bake at 350 degrees for 1½ hours. Uncover and bake at 375 degrees for another 1½ hours.

Garlic is always a many splendored thing.

THE DENVER POST

4

CROISSANTS D'AIL

BARBARA SPELLMAN, Morgan Hill, CA

Barbara Spellman, a home economics teacher, became a Great Garlic Contest finalist with this delightful recipe. Elegant and buttery, these lovely croissants get their appealing flavor from the creamy garlic butter that is mixed into the dough.

GARLIC BUTTER:

3   to 8 cloves fresh garlic
1   quart boiling water
4   tablespoons butter

CROISSANT DOUGH:

4   cups flour
6   tablespoons sugar
2   teaspoons salt
2   oz. yeast, softened in ½ cup warm water for about 20 minutes
1   cup water *or* milk (plus or minus a little)
¾   cup butter
1   egg

BUTTER:

Place unpeeled cloves of garlic in boiling water for 5 seconds. Drain, peel, and rinse under cold water. Bring to a boil again for 30 seconds; drain and rinse.

Pound into a smooth paste in a mortar or put through a garlic press.

Soften butter and mix with the garlic paste. Set aside.

DOUGH:

Sift together the flour, sugar, and salt in a large mixing bowl. Add the softened yeast. Gradually add the water (milk) until the mixture forms a ball (you may need to vary this 1 cup of liquid more or less depending upon the moisture level of the flour). Continue kneading in the bowl or on a lightly floured pastry cloth until a smooth, elastic dough is formed.

Place about ⅓ of the dough back in the bowl, and add the garlic butter to it. When this is mixed into the dough, add the remaining ⅔ of the dough. Mix thoroughly.

On a lightly floured cloth, roll the dough into a rectangle about ⅜-inch thick. Place ¾ cup butter (soft enough to spread) in the center of the dough. Bring each side up and over the butter. Seal the center and ends of the dough. Fold the dough into thirds; turn and roll to the size of the original rectangle. Repeat this process two more times.

Fold the dough into thirds. Allow the dough to rise at room temperature until doubled in size.

Place on a baking sheet and refrigerate 45 minutes to 1 hour, until dough is chilled. Remove from the refrigerator and roll into a rectangle about 10 inches by 20 inches. Cut into 10 rectangles about 4 inches by 5 inches. Cut each of these rectangles in half diagonally. Roll each piece of dough, beginning at the wide end; curve to crescent shape; place on an ungreased baking sheet and allow to rise until doubled in size (about 2 hours).

Paint with egg mixed with a small amount of water and bake in 400-degree oven for 10 to 15 minutes, depending upon desired brownness.

Optional: Before rolling dough into crescent shape, sprinkle with freshly chopped parsley mixed with Parmesan cheese.

Makes 20 croissants.

1980

JO'S BAKED GARLIC SOUP

JO STALLARD, Pacific Grove, CA

"I'll never live this down," teased grandmotherly Jo Stallard as she was crowned with a tiara of fresh garlic and draped in garlic wreaths. A vegetarian, Jo has turned her cooking talents to adapting recipes for meatless cooking. This delicious soup has always been a winner with her friends, she says, and so it was, too, with the 1980 Great Garlic Recipe Contest and Cook-off celebrity judges.

2	cups diced fresh tomatoes
1	can (approximately 15 oz.) garbanzo beans, undrained
4	*or* 5 summer squash, sliced
2	large onions, sliced
½	green pepper, diced
1½	cups dry white wine
4	*or* 5 cloves fresh garlic, minced
1	bay leaf
2	teaspoons salt
1	teaspoon basil
½	teaspoon paprika
1¼	cups grated Monterey Jack cheese
1	cup grated Romano cheese
1¼	cups heavy cream *or* whipping cream

Generously butter inside of 3-quart baking dish. Combine all ingredients, except cheese and cream, in dish.

Cover and bake for 1 hour at 375 degrees. Stir in cheeses and cream, lower heat to 325 degrees and bake 10 to 15 minutes longer.

Do not allow to boil. Mmmmmm—GOOD!

Serves 4–6.

Oh, that miracle clove! Not only does garlic taste good, it cures baldness and tennis elbow, too.

LAURIE BURROWS GRAD
LOS ANGELES MAGAZINE

7

MEDITERRANEAN CHICKEN BREASTS

KAREN MAHSHI, Concord, CA

*Still another mouth-watering Forty-Clove chicken.
In this original version, succulent chicken breasts are marinated in
seasoned lemon juice, lightly coated, and combined with blanched fresh garlic cloves
that are so sweet you can eat them by the handful.*

2	lemons
4	large cloves garlic, minced
1½	teaspoons salt
1	teaspoon chopped fresh oregano
¼	teaspoon freshly ground pepper
¼	cup olive oil
¼	cup safflower oil
8	supremes (breasts from 4 frying chickens, boned and skinned)
1	cup fresh grated Parmesan cheese
1	cup fine, white, fresh bread crumbs
2	cups chicken stock (canned *or* homemade)
30	to 40 garlic cloves, peeled
	Butter
1	cup dry white wine
⅓	cup minced fresh parsley leaves
	Parsley sprigs

Remove lemon zest (yellow part of peel) with vegetable peeler and mince. With wide-bladed knife, make paste of minced garlic and salt. Combine lemon zest, 2 tablespoons lemon juice, garlic paste, oregano, pepper and oil. (Alternate method: Place unminced zest and garlic cloves in food processor and process a few seconds, using steel blade. Add salt, pepper, oregano leaves and lemon juice. With processor turned on, add oils in slow stream.)

Coat chicken breasts with marinade; let stand several hours or overnight.

Remove supremes from marinade and scrape off excess. Roll chicken in mixture of Parmesan and bread crumbs. Lay coated supremes on waxed paper; allow to set 15 minutes to several hours.

Heat chicken stock to boiling and blanch the 30 to 40 garlic cloves in it for 10 minutes. Remove and drain garlic. Reserve stock for sauce, reducing to 1½ cups while chicken is baking.

Place supremes in shallow baking dish, coated with butter. Drizzle a little melted butter on each breast. Strew blanched garlic cloves over and around breasts.

Cover with foil and bake in a preheated 375-degree oven 15 to 20 minutes, or until nearly done. Remove foil and place chicken under broiler until golden brown.

Remove to heated platter and distribute the garlic around the breasts. Keep warm while preparing sauce.

Add dry white wine to juices remaining in the baking pan after chicken is removed. Deglaze pan over high heat, scraping up any brown bits clinging to bottom and sides.

Pour mixture into saucepan and reduce over high heat to ¼ cup. Add reserved chicken stock and minced parsley and reduce mixture to about 1 cup. Remove pan from heat. Add lemon juice, salt, and pepper to taste.

Pour some sauce over chicken breasts and garnish platter with sprigs of parsley. Pass remaining sauce in a pitcher.

Makes 8 servings.

8

HELEN'S BAGGY HENNY

HELEN HEADLEE, South San Francisco, CA

"So pretty with their golden brown glaze and even better to eat. Everyone will think that you spent all day slaving over a hot oven," says Helen Headlee, two-time finalist in the Great Garlic Recipe Contest and Cook-off.

1	pkg. (6 oz.) long grain and wild rice mixture (*or* use your favorite stuffing)
2	cups water
4	to 6 Cornish game hens (one per person)
½	cup soy sauce
½	cup honey
½	teaspoon paprika
1½	teaspoons salt
8	cloves fresh garlic, peeled and sliced
3	slices ginger root, peeled and cut coarsely
2	cups flour
4	to 6 small brown paper bags (lunch size)
	Salad oil

Cook rice using 2 cups water for 20 minutes. Allow to cool. Wash and dry hens. Cook soy sauce, honey, seasonings, garlic, and ginger together, stirring until it comes to a boil. Remove from heat.

Put flour into a large paper or plastic bag. Place hens in the bag and shake until hens are coated with flour. Roll the floured hens in the soy mixture or spoon this sauce on, coating the entire hens thoroughly.

Put small paper bags on a cookie sheet (do one at a time). Pour salad oil over the bag, saturating it well. (This is the messy part and you'll say "Ugh," but keep on.) When all the bags are soaked with oil set them aside. Wipe excess oil off cookie sheet.

Spoon the cooked rice (or stuffing) into the hen. Slip the hen into the oiled paper bag. Staple the end shut. Place the bagged hens on cookie racks on the cookie sheet.

Bake at 350 degrees for 1 hour. Split bag open. If not brown enough, return to oven for a few more minutes.

Serves 4–6.

SCALLOPS GILROIX

JAMES JEFFERSON, Los Gatos, CA

An aromatic sauce, thick and bubbling, enfolds tender scallops in this luscious appetizer that's served in individual bowls. If used as an entree, double the recipe.

Melt butter in a small saucepan. Add garlic, garlic salt, tarragon, pepper medley, and wine. Stir well and bring to a boil.

Add scallops and sauté 3 minutes. Thicken the sauce with cornstarch. Reduce heat. When mixture stops boiling, stir in the sour cream.

Serve in small bowls.

Serves 4.

6	tablespoons butter
3	large cloves fresh garlic, finely chopped
½	teaspoon garlic salt
½	teaspoon tarragon, crushed
½	teaspoon pepper medley
¼	cup white wine
½	lb. fresh scallops, rinsed and drained
1	teaspoon cornstarch
½	cup sour cream

9

GARLIC MUSHROOM CASSEROLE

R. J. HARRIS, Gilroy, CA

Plump, fresh mushrooms are stuffed with a hardy filling that includes plenty of garlic and a surprise ingredient: chopped almonds. For a vegetarian meal it is also quite palatable prepared with soy paste as a substitute for the beef.

16	large fresh mushrooms for stuffing
½	lb. small mushrooms
1	cup finely diced fresh garlic
1	cup chopped almonds
½	lb. butter
1	lb. ground beef
2	cups seasoned bread crumbs
1	cup grated Swiss *or* Mozzarella Cheese
½	cup grated Parmesan cheese

Trim large mushrooms; discard ends. Remove stems and chop together with small mushrooms. Sauté garlic, chopped mushrooms and almonds in half the butter until well done. Add beef and cook until done. Add 1½ cups bread crumbs and mix thoroughly.

Line bottom of greased casserole with 8 large mushrooms (open side up). Press sautéed mixture firmly over mushrooms. Use remaining 8 large mushrooms to cover sautéed mixture (place open side down). Sprinkle with grated Swiss or Mozzarella cheese, remaining bread crumbs and Parmesan cheese. Dot with remaining half of the butter.

Bake at 350 degrees for 35 minutes or until mushrooms are tender.

Serves 8.

Note: Can use soy paste instead of ground meat. Add extra ½ lb. butter for moisture.

MOCK OYSTER STIR-FRY

LEONARD BRILL, San Francisco, CA

An imaginative combination of ingredients transforms this inexpensive, quick-to-prepare dish into a delectable treat. You won't even miss the oysters.

3	tablespoons oil (½ vegetable, ½ sesame)
3	to 4 cloves fresh garlic, chopped
2	cups sliced zucchini
½	cup sliced fresh mushrooms
2	cups tofu, cut in ½-inch cubes
1	tablespoon soy sauce
⅓	cup oyster sauce
	Sesame seeds

Heat oil in wok or frying pan over medium-high heat. Add garlic, zucchini, and mushrooms. Stir-fry until zucchini starts to brown (about 2 minutes). Add tofu and toss. Reduce heat to low-medium.

Mix soy sauce and oyster sauce and pour over. Toss and cook, covered, 2 to 3 minutes. Remove cover and cook another minute or so until sauce thickens.

Sprinkle with sesame seeds.

Serves 4.

10

RED BELLIES

BOB DIXON, Santa Cruz, CA

These little tomato red bellies are chock-full with a delightful filling of bulgur wheat, crunchy nuts, and fresh seasonings. Spoon on the Green Walnut and Garlic Butter for the final treat.

1	cup chicken stock
½	cup bulgur wheat
4	firm, large, fresh tomatoes
8	large cloves fresh garlic
½	cup chopped walnuts
3	tablespoons olive oil
¼	cup fresh parsley, chopped
3	tablespoons fresh basil, minced (*or* ½ teaspoon dried)
2	tablespoons minced watercress (optional)
1	tablespoon Worcestershire sauce
	Juice of 1 lemon
	Salt to taste
	Green Walnut and Garlic Butter (recipe below)

GREEN WALNUT AND GARLIC BUTTER:

4	cloves fresh garlic, minced and mashed
6	walnut halves, minced
1	tablespoon olive oil
½	cup butter (creamed)
4	large spinach leaves, minced
2	tablespoons minced basil
	Dash of Tabasco

Pour heated chicken stock over bulgur. Cover and let stand 1 hour.

Slice top off each tomato. Remove pulp and reserve. Place tomatoes upside down on paper towel to drain.

Sauté garlic and walnuts in 2 tablespoons of olive oil over low heat for 2 to 3 minutes.

In a medium bowl combine bulgur, walnuts, garlic, parsley, basil, watercress, Worcestershire sauce, lemon juice, salt and reserved tomato pulp. Fill tomato shells with mixture and sprinkle with remaining olive oil.

Place in an oiled dish and bake at 350 degrees for 15 to 20 minutes. Add a generous tablespoon of the Green Walnut and Garlic Butter on top of each tomato and return to oven for 2 or 3 minutes.

BUTTER:

Sauté garlic and walnuts for 2 minutes in olive oil. Mash well. Combine butter with all ingredients and chill until needed.

11

CALZONE

DAVID LEHMANN, Palo Alto, CA

Choose your own filling for this huge, hearty turnover. A type of folded over pizza, it was a favorite of many tasters in the Great Garlic Contest and Cook-off audience. Can be eaten either hot or cold, and also packs well for a picnic.

PIZZA DOUGH:

2	envelopes active dry yeast
1	teaspoon sugar
¼	cup warm water (100 degrees)
4	cups warm water
⅓	cup olive oil
1	teaspoon salt
1½	cups nonfat dry milk powder
12	cups unbleached white flour

PIZZA SAUCE:

1	head fresh garlic
⅓	cup olive oil
1	can (28 oz.) heavy tomato puree
1	can (28 oz.) peeled Italian tomatoes, diced *or* 2 lbs. fresh peeled tomatoes, diced
1½	tablespoons dry whole basil
1½	tablespoons dry whole oregano
½	teaspoon salt
1	teaspoon crushed hot red pepper

FILLINGS:

Cheeses: wholemilk Mozzarella, ricotta, Bel Paese, Parmesan, Romano.

Ham (prosciutto) *or* sausage, sliced thin.

Onions and/*or* mushrooms, sliced and sautéed with garlic.

Marinated artichoke hearts *or* black olives.

DOUGH:

Stir first 3 ingredients together in a warm quart bowl in a warm kitchen. Set aside to proof. The yeast will start working quickly if it is good.

Stir next 4 ingredients and 6 cups of the flour together in a large warm bowl. Then add the yeast mixture and stir in 3 more cups of flour slowly. Continue to add flour gradually, stirring very vigorously. When dough is too stiff to stir, dump out on a lightly floured board and knead until smooth and elastic (10–15 minutes), adding just enough flour to keep dough from sticking. The 12-cup estimate of flour can vary greatly. You can use half whole wheat flour, but the dough will not be as elastic. This should make about 6 pounds of dough.

Cut into ½-pound pieces for individual calzone or pizzas. Form into balls, rub with olive oil, and allow to rise in a warm place on plates or a pan large enough so they won't touch and stick together. Let rise until doubled in size.

SAUCE:

Separate and clean the cloves of garlic. Slice them thinly, crosswise. Place with oil in a kettle large enough to hold all the sauce. Heat gently until the garlic is sizzling in the oil. Do not let the garlic brown.

Pour the tomato puree and the tomatoes into the kettle. Stir in the basil, oregano, salt and red pepper. Simmer 15 minutes, stirring often, and allow to cool.

Enough for a dozen individual calzone or 3 to 4 large pizzas.

12

MAKING CALZONE:

To form a calzone crust, take a ½-pound ball of risen pizza dough and place on a floured board. Pound out flat with hands, being careful to keep the round shape. Use a rolling pin if you need to. The dough should be evenly thin and as big around as a dinner plate.

Spread pizza sauce over the whole dough, except for an inch border around the edge. Put grated cheeses and other fillings on half the sauced area. Use any combinations you like, but be careful not to pile too much on.

Fold the other side of the dough over the fillings, and seal the edges together by pressing the borders firmly with your fingers. Rub a little olive oil over the top of the calzone. Put a tablespoon of sauce or cheese on the very top for decoration, or to denote what is inside.

Bake on an oiled pan or baking sheet in a 450-degree oven until the crust is golden brown on sides and bottom (8 to 18 minutes, depending on your oven).

Each calzone will make a meal for someone hungry. Serve with wine or beer and a green salad. Calzone pack well to be eaten cold on a picnic.

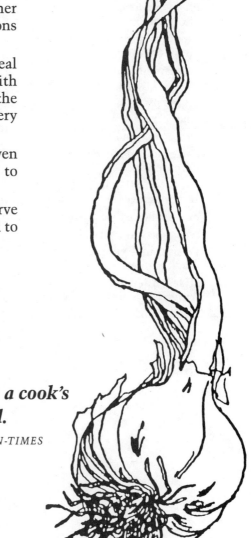

Garlic is a cook's best friend.
CHICAGO SUN-TIMES

13

COUNTRY PICNIC LOAF

JACKIE HOWARD, Morgan Hill, CA

Sourdough bread is transformed into a family-pleasing sandwich loaf. An imaginative entree for a hot summer day, it can be prepared ahead of time and either reheated or served cold for a picnic outing.

1	loaf rounded sourdough French bread
3	cloves fresh garlic, chopped fine
1	medium-sized red onion, chopped fine
4	tablespoons olive oil
6	eggs, whipped
1	whole green pepper, coarsely chopped
1	can (3 oz.) small shrimp
¾	cup chopped leftover ham *or* pork
8	slices of Italian hard salami, diced
2	or 3 dashes garlic powder
1	teaspoon chile powder
	Dash coarse ground black pepper
6	slices Muenster *or* American Swiss Cheese

Cut sourdough bread in half horizontally and scoop out enough bread on upper and lower sections with a sharp knife to form a dishlike loaf. (Reserve removed bread to add to a meat loaf or for making croutons.)

Sprinkle bottom loaf inside with garlic and onion; then drizzle olive oil over all. Set aside.

In nonstick fry pan sprayed with nonstick vegetable shortening, sauté whipped eggs; add green pepper, then stir in shrimp, ham or pork and salami. When the eggs are almost set, add garlic powder, chile powder, and pepper. (Add no salt as salami and spices will be adequate.) Stir until all ingredients are hot and the eggs have set.

Spoon mixture over garlic and onions in bottom half of loaf, filling completely. Cover with overlapping slices of cheese, and top with remaining half loaf. Wrap tightly in foil and keep warm. This can be made ahead of time and then warmed in 350-degree oven for about 30 minutes.

Slice in pie-shaped wedges and serve with fresh fruit in season or a crisp green salad with a garlic, olive oil, and fresh lemon juice dressing.

Makes 6 to 8 servings.

14

GOLDEN GARLIC CLOUDS

JEANNE HOWARD, Monterey Park, CA

*F*ascinating Yorkshire pudding popovers with pizazz! A quick, glorious
accompaniment to roasts, steaks and stews. Makes even the
simplest of meat dishes seem extra special.

	Shortening, bacon grease *or* **fat drippings**
2	**eggs**
½	**cup whole milk**
6	**or more cloves fresh garlic** *or* **1 teaspoon garlic powder**
1	**teaspoon dried bouquet garni, well crushed**
½	**cup all-purpose flour, unsifted**
½	**teaspoon salt**
⅛	**teaspoon baking powder**

Preheat oven to 450 degrees. Be sure all ingredients are room temperature.

Prepare large muffin pan (preferably cast iron) by greasing generously with either shortening, bacon grease, or fat drippings from roast. Heat in oven until fat *spits*.

Beat eggs well. Add milk and mix together either by electric mixer or by hand.

If using fresh garlic, peel and put through garlic press and add the resulting juice. If using garlic powder, sift with dry ingredients.

Sift dry ingredients together, add to milk mixture and beat until thoroughly blended.

Remove muffin pan from oven and quickly pour in batter to about ½ full. Immediately return to oven and bake 20 minutes *without opening oven*.

Makes about 8 large clouds. For double recipe, double all ingredients except use only 3 eggs (not 4).

The secret in the preparation is the preheating of the pans. The secret in the eating is the delicious surprise of the garlic and herbs.

15

1981

*G*arlic is to Gilroy
what Mardi Gras is to New Orleans ...
LOS ANGELES HERALD-EXAMINER

MOCK CAVIAR

BARRY WERTZ, British Columbia, Canada

Simulate elegant caviar with an imaginative imitation nestled in an iced bowl. Serve with lemon or set up with finely chopped eggs, tomato, and onion.

Peel and crush garlic. Drain and mash anchovy fillets. Drain olives. Halve, seed, peel, and mash avocados. Combine all ingredients.

Turn into iced bowl. Serve as spread for thin crackers or toast.

Makes 3 cups.

Note: To store, squeeze lemon juice over top, seal with clear plastic wrap and refrigerate.

3	large cloves fresh garlic
1	can (2 oz.) anchovy fillets
2	cups chopped ripe olives
2	large ripe avocados

GARLIC SHRIMP SALAD

LOVELLE OBERHOLZER, Concord, CA

Delicate pink shrimp and luscious green avocados and artichoke hearts are featured in this salad which is an adaptation of one served all over the Mediterranean area. For variation, chicken can be substituted for the shrimp.

9	cloves fresh garlic
¼	cup butter *or* margarine
1½ to 2 lbs.	large shelled, deveined shrimp
2	large tomatoes
2	medium cucumbers
3	green onions
4	cooked artichoke hearts, halved
½	cup salad oil
¼	cup lemon juice
½	tablespoon crushed sweet basil
¼	tablespoon dried dill weed
	Salt and pepper
1	avocado

Peel and mince 6 cloves garlic. Melt butter in a heavy skillet. Add minced garlic and sauté over medium heat until light golden. Add shrimp and cook 2 or 3 minutes, turning continuously, just until they are pink. Remove from heat.

Break shrimp into bite-sized pieces into a large bowl and add the cooked garlic. Remove skin, seed and chop tomatoes. Peel, seed and chop cucumber. Chop onions and halve artichoke hearts. Combine vegetables with shrimp.

Mince remaining 3 cloves garlic and combine with oil, lemon juice, herbs and salt and pepper to taste. Beat until blended, then pour over shrimp mixture, mixing well.

Halve, remove seed and skin and dice avocado into salad mixture. Serve in small bowls with crusty French bread and butter.

Makes 6 to 8 servings.

17

GARLIC-CHICKEN PHYLLO ROLLS

MARY JANE HIMEL, Palo Alto, CA

This recipe turns out best when prosciutto is used. Look for it in an Italian grocery or deli if not available at your supermarket. It adds considerable flavor. Also, be sure to keep the phyllo dough moist as you work with it. Keep it covered with a dampened towel.

2	heads fresh garlic
½	cup dry white wine
½	cup water
	Juice of 1 lemon
¼	teaspoon salt
1	lb. boned, skinned chicken breasts
6	sheets phyllo
¼	cup butter, melted
2½	oz. thinly sliced prosciutto *or* 3 slices boiled ham, halved
2	cups grated Swiss cheese

Separate garlic into cloves and drop into boiling water. Simmer 1 minute, drain, and peel.

Bring wine, water, lemon juice, and salt to simmer in large saucepan. Add chicken and garlic. Cook at a bare simmer, turning occasionally, just until chicken is cooked.

Remove chicken and continue cooking garlic until tender, then drain. Cut chicken into large chunks and divide into 6 portions.

Lay out 1 phyllo sheet, brush half with butter and fold in half crosswise. Brush with butter again.

Top with a portion of chicken and garlic cloves lightly mashed with a fork along a short end. Top with ⅙ of the prosciutto, and ⅓ cup cheese.

Fold in the sides and roll up. Repeat with remaining phyllo sheets. Work quickly so phyllo doesn't dry out. Place rolls on lightly greased baking sheet and brush them with butter.

Bake at 400 degrees about 20 minutes, until golden.

Makes 6 rolls.

18

GARLIC GODDESS CHEESE PIE

JACQUELINE BEARDSLEY, San Francisco, CA

This nutritious filling nestled in a novel potato crust makes a rich, tempting pie which is not only healthy but sooooo good!

POTATO CRUST:
2 large raw potatoes
½ teaspoon salt
1 large beaten egg

FILLING:
3 large cloves fresh garlic
1 green onion
2 bunches asparagus
15 medium-sized mushrooms
3 tablespoons butter
½ teaspoon salt
½ teaspoon dried basil
   Dash thyme
2¼ heaping cups grated white Cheddar cheese
2 large eggs
¼ cup milk

POTATO CRUST:

Preheat oven to hot (400 degrees).

Pare and grate potatoes. Combine with salt and turn into a colander. Let drain 10 minutes, then squeeze out excess moisture. Combine with egg. Pat into oiled 9-inch pie pan to make a crust.

Bake in preheated oven 40 to 45 minutes.

FILLING:

Peel and crush garlic; trim and chop onion. Trim and chop asparagus tips and mushrooms. Sauté garlic and onion in butter a few minutes. Add asparagus and mushrooms along with seasonings. Cover and cook 10 minutes, stirring occasionally.

Spread half the cheese into the baked crust, then the vegetable sauté. Cover with remaining cheese. Beat eggs with milk and pour over the pie.

Bake in moderately hot oven, 375 degrees, 35 to 40 minutes.

Makes one 9-inch pie.

19

PESTO QUICHE

ANAHIT LEMON, Berkeley, CA

Calling garlic "a staple of life" this Cook-off finalist whipped up a classic pesto sauce and combined it with freshly laid duck eggs and cheeses in creating her savory quiche.

PESTO:

4	cloves fresh garlic
1	cup coarsely chopped fresh basil
¼	teaspoon salt
¼	teaspoon pepper, freshly ground
2	tablespoons pine nuts *or* walnuts
¼	cup olive oil
½	cup grated Parmesan cheese
2	tablespoons melted butter

QUICHE:

1	deep dish (9-inch) pie shell
4	cloves fresh garlic
1	large onion
3	tablespoons butter
3	large eggs
1	cup milk
½	cup ricotta cheese
¼	cup prepared pesto (see recipe above)
1½	cups grated Parmesan cheese

PESTO:

Peel and crush garlic. Turn into blender along with basil, salt, pepper, and pine nuts *or* walnuts. Blend at high speed. Alternately blend in olive oil and grated Parmesan cheese. Stir in melted butter. Set aside.

QUICHE:

Prepare or purchase pie shell. Partially bake shell in a 350-degree oven for 5 minutes.

Peel and finely chop garlic and onion. Sauté in butter until translucent.

Lightly beat eggs. Mix milk with ricotta, then combine with eggs, garlic, onion and ¼ cup of prepared pesto. Turn into crust and sprinkle Parmesan evenly over top.

Bake in top of oven at 350 degrees for about 40 minutes, until puffed and lightly browned.

Makes one 9-inch quiche.

The soul of pesto may be basil, but its heart is garlic.

PITTSBURGH PRESS

FETTUCCINE GLORIOSA

RUDY and GLORIA MELONE, Gilroy, CA

*Guaranteed to please the gourmet palate, this 1981 first place winner
was created when Rudy Melone was preparing calamari one evening and his wife, Gloria,
came home with fresh mussels. They adapted, blended both sauces together
and improvised this fabulous seafood fettuccine. Worth every minute it takes!
It helps to have two cooks in the kitchen, one who prepares the moules
and the second who prepares the calamari.*

MOULES: (Mussels)

¾	cube butter
3	to 4 cloves fresh garlic, peeled and diced
1	medium-size onion *or* 5 to 6 shallots, diced
8	sprigs parsley, chopped fine
18	to 24 fresh mussels or clams (or combination), scrubbed clean
1	cup dry white wine

CALAMARI: (Squid)

⅓	cup olive oil
6	to 12 cloves fresh garlic peeled and crushed
2	lbs. calamari, cleaned and cut into 2-inch strips
2	tablespoons oregano
1	cup dry white wine
1	lemon, halved
1	can (8 oz.) tomato sauce
2	shakes Tabasco sauce, to taste

FETTUCCINE:

2	teaspoons salt
	Water
2	tablespoons olive oil
1	lb. white or green fettuccine (preferably homemade)
	Parmesan cheese

MOULES:

In pan with lid, melt butter and add garlic, onions, and parsley. When onions are translucent, add mussels. Cover and when mussels start to open, add the wine. Stir and remove from stove when mussels have opened. If any do not open they should be removed and discarded.

CALAMARI:

Heat olive oil in skillet; add garlic and cook until garlic is golden brown. Add calamari, cook for about 1 minute, add oregano, and then the wine. Cook about ½ minute longer, squeeze juice of both lemon halves over the mixture and, for good measure, throw in the lemon halves. Add the tomato sauce and Tabasco, and simmer for about 1 minute.

Combine the mussels and calamari to create the sauce.

FETTUCCINE:

In large pot, bring salted water to a rapid boil. Add olive oil and then the fettucine. When the fettuccine is cooked *al dente*, strain fettuccine and place on a large pasta platter. Mix with the combined sauce. Arrange the mussels around the platter, decorate with sprigs of parsley, sprinkle liberally with freshly grated Parmesan cheese and serve.

Serves 4 to 6.

21

BACON-GREENS-AND-GARLIC BREAD

PATRICIA BISSINGER, Livermore, CA

The garlic in this fragrant bread is baked right in, so 1981 finalist Patricia Bissinger gives a warning with her recipe: "When the aroma of garlic perfumes the air you can anticipate company in the kitchen, if there is anyone else in the house, so be prepared for group participation until the last crumbs disappear."

2	envelopes active dry yeast
1	teaspoon sugar
½	cup warm water
½	cup fresh parsley
½	cup fresh basil
1½	cups buttermilk
4	pieces thick-sliced lean bacon
6	cloves fresh garlic
¼	cup bacon drippings
5	to 5½ cups unbleached flour
2½	teaspoons salt
¼	teaspoon black pepper, freshly ground
1	large egg, beaten
1	egg white
2	teaspoons sesame seeds

Combine yeast, sugar, and warm water in large mixing bowl. Let stand about 5 minutes until yeast is bubbly.

Meanwhile, chop parsley and basil fine. Heat buttermilk just until lukewarm. Dice bacon fine and fry until crispy. Peel and mince garlic. Add to ¼ cup bacon drippings and sauté a few seconds until the aroma of garlic perfumes the air; set aside.

Add 2 cups flour to yeast mixture along with buttermilk, bacon-garlic drippings mixture, parsley, basil, salt, pepper and whole egg. Beat hard with a spoon until thick and elastic. Continue to beat in enough of the remaining flour to make a firm dough. Knead on a well-floured surface until smooth and elastic.

Place in a greased bowl, turning to grease top. Cover and let rise in warm oven about 20 minutes. (To warm oven, turn oven to lowest setting for 1 minute, then turn off.)

Punch down dough, divide into 2 parts and shape into 12-inch-long loaves or into round loaves. Place on greased cookie sheet. Brush with egg white and sprinkle with sesame seeds. Slash top of loaves every 1½ inches. Cover and let rise until doubled, about 30 minutes.

Bake in moderately hot oven, 375 degrees, for 25 to 30 minutes, until golden brown and hollow sounding when tapped on bottom. Cool on wire rack. Serve with whipped butter and a smile.

Makes 2 loaves.

22

SAVORY ITALIAN SEASONING SALT

MRS. DOMENI ROMANO, Fresno, CA

*Italians are great users of garlic in their cooking. Mrs. Romano
has developed this recipe not only for her own use
but to give as a small gift to friends and relatives
who are also creative cooks.*

With blender turned on at low speed, add ingredients in order listed. Cover and turn on high speed to pulverize and blend well.

Store in shaker container with tight lid.

Use for seasoning steaks, roasts, vegetables, soups, stews, and salads, adding seasoning to suit taste.

Makes about 1 cup.

4	whole dried red chile peppers
¼	cup dehydrated minced garlic
½	cup dehydrated minced onion
¼	cup dried oregano leaves
¼	cup dried basil leaves
¼	cup dried parsley leaves
¼	cup salt
2	tablespoons dried rosemary (optional)

SPINACH PESTO

PENNY LOCKHART, Gilroy, CA

*This recipe may seem a heresy to the pesto purist, but by using
readily available fresh spinach and parsley in this full-flavored sauce,
it can be prepared and enjoyed the year round. It (like pesto)
is delicious over almost anything: pasta, mushrooms,
French bread, sautéed vegetables, even liver.*

6	cloves fresh garlic
1	bunch fresh spinach
1	cup fresh parsley leaves
⅔	cup freshly grated Parmesan cheese
½	cup walnut pieces
4	flat anchovy fillets
1	tablespoon dried tarragon
1	teaspoon dried basil
1	teaspoon salt
½	teaspoon pepper
¼	teaspoon anise *or* fennel seeds
1	cup olive oil

Peel and crush garlic. Wash, dry and chop spinach. Trim and discard stems from parsley.

Turn all ingredients except oil into food processor fitted with the steel blade. Blend until mixture is smooth. With motor running, add the oil in a thin stream (as when making mayonnaise). When all oil has been added, taste and add additional seasoning as desired.

Cover and refrigerate. Sauce will keep about 1 week.

Makes about 2 cups.

23

1982

*L*et's face it, is there a mortal soul who can deny that
this cousin of the onion is not one of the most
important seasoning agents known to man?

HOME ECONOMICS READING SERVICE
WASHINGTON, D.C.

TEXAS SURPRISE

KAREN MAHSHI, Concord, CA

A̶nother two-time finalist in the recipe contest, this creative cook devised a recipe guaranteed to delight garlic lovers everywhere. Whole cloves are cooked inside spicy meatballs, which can be prepared ahead and frozen before baking, to have on hand to prepare for a few drop-in friends or a crowd. If you freeze the unbaked appetizers, do not thaw, just add 5 to 10 minutes to the baking time.

50	to 60 gloves fresh garlic, peeled
12	oz. sharp Cheddar cheese
⅓	cup fresh parsley leaves (stems removed)
1	to 2 jalapeño peppers (optional)
6	cloves fresh garlic
6	oz. hot pork sausage
6	oz. mild pork sausage
2¼	cups buttermilk baking mix

Blanch 50 to 60 cloves garlic in boiling water 3 to 4 minutes. Drain and set aside to cool.

In food processor fitted with shredding disc, grate cheese. Remove and set aside. Allow cheese and sausage to come to room temperature before mixing.

In dry food processor bowl, chop parsley and peppers, if used, using steel blade. Use garlic press or side of wide-bladed knife to crush 6 cloves garlic. Add to processor, along with sausages and baking mix. Process until well mixed. Add cheese, and process only until well combined.

Shape into 50 to 60 small balls, inserting a whole blanched garlic clove in each. At this point, balls may be frozen for baking at a later time.

To bake at once, place balls on ungreased baking sheet. Bake at 325 degrees 20 to 25 minutes or until golden brown.

Serve hot as an appetizer, plain or with a bowl of plain yogurt for dipping.

Makes 50 to 60 appetizers.

25

SCANDINAVIAN TRIPE SALAD

ALICE GRAY, Berkeley, CA

Long, gentle cooking brings out the flavor of this delicacy, which is prepared here in the Scandinavian manner with yogurt, sour cream, and vinegar, laced with the bite of fresh garlic. The cheesecloth sack, by the way, used for holding the garlic is not a necessity, only a convenience for retrieving the cloves for mashing.

1	lb. tripe
2	quarts cold water
½	lemon
1	teaspoon salt
4	to 6 cloves fresh garlic, unpeeled
½	cup sour cream
½	cup plain yogurt
2	tablespoons white wine vinegar
1	teaspoon sugar
¼	teaspoon white pepper
	Salt to taste
	Minced chives

Rinse tripe in cold water, drain, and place in large saucepan with 2 quarts cold water. Squeeze juice from lemon over tripe and drop in the peel. Add salt and bring gently to boil, turn heat to low and simmer until tender, 20 minutes to 2 hours, depending on tripe.

Meanwhile, tie garlic cloves in a little cheesecloth sack, drop into kettle and cook until very tender, at least 20 minutes.

Remove garlic, cool sufficiently to handle and squeeze the garlic out of its peel into a medium-sized bowl. Add sour cream, yogurt, vinegar, sugar, and pepper and mix well. Chill.

When tripe is tender, rinse in cold water, drain and cool. Cut into coarse or medium julienne strips and mix with the dressing. Add salt to taste, mound into a serving bowl and chill.

At serving time, sprinkle with chopped chives. Serve as an hors d'oeuvre or as the main course of a light lunch.

Makes 4 servings.

26

101 GARLIC CHICKEN

Winner of the Prize for Best Recipe Using Most Garlic, 1982
HELEN McGLONE, Roseville, CA

*W*hen *serving this recipe to guests, invite them into the kitchen to let them count as you place the garlic cloves around the chicken. They won't believe how sweet and delicious the cooked garlic will be until they eat it!*

10	whole chicken breasts, split, boned and skinned
2	cups champagne
101	unpeeled cloves fresh garlic

Place chicken in ungreased baking pan, 12 × 16 or 18 inches. Sprinkle with salt and pepper and pour champagne over. Place garlic cloves around and between chicken pieces. Cover pan with foil.

Bake at 350 degrees for 1½ hours.

Remove chicken to large serving platter and place garlic around chicken. Tell guests to suck the garlic out of its skin, that it is deliciously sweet.

Makes 20 servings.

FLANK STEAK OLÉ

SANDY HOILES, Sunnyvale, CA

*T*his *recipe was named by the happy group who first sampled it and exclaimed "Olé!" Don't worry about small chunks of tamale which might fall out of the steak rolls; they add an interesting texture to the sauce.*

Stretch steak gently without tearing to a rectangular shape. Press 3 cloves garlic over meat, sprinkle with salt, pepper and chili powder. Crumble tamales over steak, spreading to within 1 inch of edges. Roll up, making a firm roll but not too tight and tie with string at intervals or secure with skewers. Dust with flour, shaking off excess.

Heat oil in Dutch oven or heavy pan with cover and brown roll on all sides over medium-high heat. Reduce heat to low.

Pour tomato sauce over roll. Measure wine into tomato sauce can and pour into tamale can with its reserved sauce. Press remaining 7 cloves garlic into this sauce, stir, and pour *around* roll not over it.

Cover and simmer until tender, about 2 to 2½ hours.

Remove from heat and remove string or skewers, disturbing topping as little as possible. Sprinkle with cheese and return to low heat. Cover and cook until cheese melts, about 20 minutes.

Place roll on serving platter and cut into 1-inch slices. Pass sauce separately in gravy boat or bowl.

Makes 4 servings.

1	flank steak (2 to 2½ lbs.), tenderized
10	cloves fresh garlic (about 1 head)
½	teaspoon salt
¼	teaspoon pepper
1	teaspoon chili powder
1	can (15 oz.) tamales, papers discarded and sauce reserved
¼	cup flour
2	to 3 tablespoons olive oil
1	can (8 oz.) tomato sauce
1	cup red table wine
⅓	cup grated Parmesan cheese

27

LAMB SHANKS WITH BARLEY AND GARLIC

JOHN ROBINSON, Granada Hills, CA

This hearty award-winning entree which won a third prize for its originator requires 30 cloves of fresh garlic to achieve its robust flavor. If you'd like even more garlic flavor, stud the lamb with slivers of fresh garlic before cooking.

LAMB:
4	lamb shanks
¼	cup *each* butter and olive oil
½	cup *each* red table wine and water
½	teaspoon rosemary (more if desired)
30	cloves fresh garlic, peeled

BARLEY:
½ to ¾	lb. fresh mushrooms, sliced
½	cup butter
1½	cups pearl barley
2½ to 3½	cups beef bouillon
2	tablespoons mint jelly

LAMB:

In ovenproof pan with tight fitting lid, brown lamb on all sides in butter and olive oil.

Remove lamb, stir wine and water into pan and heat, scraping bottom and sides of pan. Replace lamb and sprinkle with rosemary. Add at least 30 cloves garlic.

Put a sheet of foil over top, then the tight fitting lid to seal thoroughly. Bake at 350 degrees for 1½ hours.

Prepare barley.

BARLEY:

Sauté mushrooms in ¼ cup butter and set aside.

Brown barley in remaining ¼ cup butter until golden brown. Mix in mushrooms, turn into casserole, and add 2½ cups beef bouillon.

Cover and bake 30 minutes at 350 degrees. Add more bouillon as needed, about 1 cup, and cook, uncovered, until liquid is absorbed and barley is done.

To serve, arrange lamb shanks around edges of serving platter. Add garlic cloves to barley, and heap in center of platter. Stir mint jelly into liquid remaining, cook 3 to 5 minutes, and spoon over lamb.

Makes 4 servings.

28

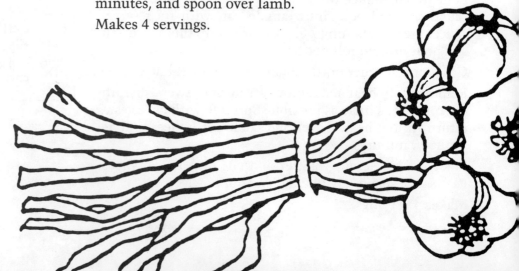

FETTUCCINE GARLI-MARI
BYRON RUDY, Livermore, CA

A zesty calamari sauce using two heads of fresh garlic tops off this rich creamy fettuccine concoction. It was good enough to win second place for the chef who created it in the third annual Great Garlic Recipe Contest.

2	heads fresh garlic, about 30 cloves
2	lbs. calamari
4½	tablespoons butter
1	tablespoon olive oil
¼	cup packed finely chopped parsley
2	tablespoons dry white table wine
12	oz. fettuccine
½	cup heavy cream
2½	oz. freshly grated Parmesan cheese

Put garlic cloves through press.

Clean calamari, fillet and cut into ¼-inch strips.

Sauté garlic in 1½ tablespoons butter and olive oil, stirring often, until soft and golden. Add calamari and cook over medium-low heat, turning often, until strips curl. Reduce heat, add wine and parsley, and cook 2 minutes longer.

Meanwhile, cook fettuccine as package directs (coordinate cooking time with calamari, so both are done at once); drain.

Melt remaining 3 tablespoons butter in a hot serving bowl, combine butter, heavy cream and Parmesan cheese, and mix together. Add fettuccine and calamari, and mix together with pasta forks. Serve immediately on warm serving plates. Makes 6 servings.

HUNGARIAN SALAMI
AMBER BURNEY, Ventura, CA

"I'm a garlic fiend," says Amber Burney. "I'm very sure I use 10 heads a month— not cloves, heads." This scrumptious salami contains eight fresh garlic cloves and when chilled, resembles a firm paté. Delicious!

Combine all ingredients and mix well. Shape into 2 logs, each about 10 inches long. Cover and refrigerate overnight.

Uncover, place on broiling pan and bake in a very slow oven 225 degrees for 2 hours. Cool before slicing.

Makes 2 logs salami.

8	cloves fresh garlic, minced
2	lbs. ground beef (33% fat)
1	tablespoon Hungarian paprika
1	tablespoon salt
1	tablespoon coarsely ground black pepper
1	tablespoon onion powder
1	tablespoon dill seed
1	tablespoon chopped fresh basil (*or* 1 teaspoon dry)
1	teaspoon liquid smoke
1	teaspoon whole coriander seed
1	teaspoon whole pickling spice
1	teaspoon mustard seed

29

ARTICHOKES ALLA ROSINA

Winner of 1982 Recipe Contest
ROSINA WILSON, Albany, CA

This winning recipe from a very talented lady combines steamed artichokes and whole cloves of garlic which are dipped in a tantalizing basil-laced aioli sauce, then drawn between the teeth to extract the pulp and sauce simultaneously. Thoroughly delightful! The name for the sauce, "Baioli," came from her daughter. It's a contraction of basil and aioli. Substitute fresh tarragon for "Taioli," fresh dill for "Daioli," or parsley for "Paioli."

6	medium artichokes
6	large heads fresh garlic
1	large lemon, halved
½	teaspoon salt
½	cup olive oil

BAIOLI SAUCE:

4	to 6 cloves fresh garlic, peeled
2	eggs yolks
3	tablespoons lemon juice
1	teaspoon Dijon-style mustard
½	teaspoon salt
1	cup olive oil
½	cup fresh basil leaves

Clean artichokes and place in a large kettle. Peel off outer papery skin from garlic, leaving heads intact. Nestle garlic heads among artichokes.

Add water to cover artichokes halfway, squeeze in juice from lemons, and tuck in the lemon peels. Add salt, and pour olive oil over. Bring to a boil, and simmer 45 to 60 minutes, until tender, depending on size of artichokes. Drain well.

Serve warm or cold, with Baioli Sauce. The garlic heads will be soft enough to eat like the artichokes, picking off cloves, pulling out pulp between the teeth, and discarding skin.

Makes 6 servings.

BAIOLI SAUCE:

In blender jar, place 4 to 6 cloves fresh garlic, peeled, 2 egg yolks, 3 tablespoons lemon juice, 1 tablespoon mustard and ½ teaspoon salt. Cover and blend smooth.

With blender running, remove cover and very slowly pour in 1 cup olive oil in a very thin stream. Cover blender, turn off and scrape down sides. Adjust seasoning.

Add ½ cup fresh sweet basil leaves and blend briefly, until coarsely chopped.

30

TOMATOES A LA WILLIAM

BILL SCALES, Gilroy, CA

Fresh whole tomatoes are scooped out and filled with a savory mixture of onion, sausage, garlic, and bread crumbs, then baked with their caps on until juicy and tender.

6	medium to large tomatoes
	Salt
	Garlic powder
2	lb. ground sausage meat
2	tablespoons butter
3	onions, diced
4	cloves fresh garlic, minced
1/3	bunch fresh parsley, finely chopped
1/4	cup bread crumbs

Cut tops from tomatoes and set aside. Scoop out insides of tomatoes and reserve for another use. Sprinkle insides of tomatoes with salt and garlic powder and turn upside down on paper towels to drain.

Brown sausage in buttered skillet. Drain and discard fat.

Sauté onions and garlic in butter until soft. Combine with sausage, parsley, and bread crumbs. Cook gently over medium heat 5 minutes.

Spoon into tomato shells and set tops back in place. Sprinkle lightly with additional bread crumbs.

Bake uncovered at 325 degrees 45 minutes.

Makes 6 servings.

CALIFORNIA GOURMET GARLIC LOAF

LEONA PEARCE, Carmichael, CA

This recipe for a split loaf of French bread, stuffed with artichoke hearts, cheese, sour cream, olives, and garlic makes eight generous servings of crusty, cheesy, garlicky goodness.

1	(1 lb.) long loaf sweet French bread
1/2	cup butter
6	cloves fresh garlic, crushed
1 1/2	cups sour cream
2	cups cubed Monterey Jack cheese
1/4	cup grated Parmesan cheese
2	tablespoons dried parsley flakes
2	teaspoons lemon pepper seasoning
1	can (14 oz.) artichoke hearts, drained
1	cup shredded Cheddar cheese
1	can (6 oz.) pitted ripe olives
	Tomato slices and parsley sprigs for garnish

Cut French bread in halves lengthwise. Place halves on aluminum foil-covered baking sheet. Tear out soft inner portion of bread in large chunks, leaving crusts intact.

Melt butter in large skillet and stir in garlic and sesame seeds. Add bread chunks and fry until bread is golden and butter is absorbed. Remove from heat.

Combine sour cream, Jack cheese, Parmesan cheese, parsley flakes and lemon pepper seasoning. Stir in drained artichoke hearts and toasted bread mixture; mix well.

Spoon into bread crust shells and sprinkle with Cheddar cheese. Bake at 350 degrees for 30 minutes.

Meanwhile, drain olives well. Remove bread from oven and arrange olives around edges of bread and tomato slices and parsley sprigs down center.

Makes 8 servings.

31

SOUTHERN CALIFORNIA'S BEST BREAD IN THE WEST

RITA PHISTER, Riverside, CA

The chile, garlic, and Cheddar filling in this braided bread is the surprise ingredient that brought this contestant to the finals in the 1982 Great Garlic Recipe Contest.

DOUGH:

1	envelope active dry yeast
¼	cup warm water
½	cup milk
2	eggs
¼	cup soft butter *or* margarine
3	tablespoons sugar
1½	teaspoons salt
1½	teaspoons ground cumin
3½	cups all-purpose flour
	Green Chile Filling (recipe below)
½	cup grated Cheddar cheese

GREEN CHILE FILLING:

1	large onion, chopped
8	cloves fresh garlic, chopped
1	tablespoon butter
2	cups grated Cheddar cheese
1	can (7 oz.) diced green chiles

DOUGH:

In large bowl of electric mixer, dissolve yeast in warm water.

Blend in milk, eggs, butter, sugar, salt, and cumin. Blend in 2 cups flour, 1 cup at a time. Beat on medium speed of mixer 3 minutes, scraping bowl often. With heavy-duty mixer (or with wooden spoon) blend in remaining flour to make a soft dough.

Turn out onto floured board, and knead until smooth, 5 to 10 minutes. Place in greased bowl, turn over, and cover. Let rise in warm place until doubled, about 1½ hours.

Meanwhile, prepare Green Chile Filling.

When dough has risen, punch down and turn out onto floured board. Roll to a 9×30-inch rectangle. Crumble filling over dough to within 1 inch of edges. Starting from long side, roll up tightly. Moisten edge with water and pinch together firmly to seal. Using a floured sharp knife, cut roll lengthwise in halves. Carefully turn cut sides up. Loosely twist the two strips together, keeping cut sides up. Transfer to greased and floured baking sheet, and shape to 10-inch circle. Pinch ends firmly together.

Let rise in warm place, uncovered, until puffy looking, about 45 to 60 minutes.

Bake at 375 degrees 15 minutes. Sprinkle with ½ cup Cheddar cheese and bake 5 minutes longer, until browned.

Makes 1 10-inch twist.

GREEN CHILE FILLING:

Sauté onion and garlic in butter until soft but not browned. Cool.

Mix in 2 cups Cheddar and chiles. Cover and chill.

KRUSTY GARLIC KUCHEN

PATRICIA BISSINGER, Livermore, CA

*This bread recipe is from a second-time finalist in the Recipe Contest,
a very creative cook whose entry won high praise from all who sampled it.
It is also excellent cold. "Enjoy! Enjoy!" said Ms. Bissinger,
and we did, we did!*

DOUGH:

1	envelope active dry yeast
1½	cups warm water
3	cups unbleached flour
1	cup whole wheat flour
¼	cup grated Parmesan cheese
1	egg, lightly beaten
2	tablespoons vegetable oil
1	teaspoon garlic salt

GARLIC TOPPING:

1	head fresh garlic, minced (10 to 12 cloves)
2	tablespoons vegetable oil
1	cup sour cream
2	eggs, lightly beaten
½	teaspoon salt
	Minced chives *or* green scallion tops

DOUGH:

Sprinkle yeast over warm water and let stand until bubbly.

Meanwhile, measure all remaining dough ingredients into food processor bowl. Add yeast mixture and process just until dough forms a ball.

Turn out onto floured surface and knead until dough is soft and no longer sticky. Shape into a ball, place in greased bowl, cover and let rise in warm place while preparing topping.

GARLIC TOPPING:

Peel and mince garlic cloves. Sauté 3 to 5 minutes in oil over low heat, until soft but not browned. Remove from heat and cool slightly, then combine with sour cream, eggs and salt.

Press dough into bottom and up sides of greased 10 × 15 × 1-inch pan, forming rim around edges. Crimp edge (*or* cut rim to decorate edge). Spread Garlic Topping evenly into pan and sprinkle with minced chives.

Bake at 400 degrees 20 to 24 minutes until edges are well browned and creamy garlic topping is light golden.

Serve slightly warm, cut into strips as bread or appetizer.

Makes 8 to 10 servings.

33

1983

PEOPLE ALWAYS ASK FOR THIS RECIPE PARTY DIP

BETTY SHAW, Santee, CA

The best part of this recipe is when all the dip is gone and all that is left is the bread which is soaked in all those delicious ingredients. Just break the bread up and pass it around!

1	loaf sheepherders bread
¼	lb. butter
1	bunch green onions, chopped
12	cloves fresh garlic, minced finely
1	pkg. (8 oz.) cream cheese, at room temperature
16	oz. sour cream
12	oz. Cheddar cheese, grated
1	can (10 oz.) artichoke hearts, drained and cut into quarters (water pack not marinated)
6	small French rolls, sliced thinly, but not all the way through.

Cut a hole in the top of the bread loaf 5 inches in diameter. If you wish, make a zigzag pattern to be decorative. Remove soft bread from cut portion and discard. Reserve crust to make top for loaf. Scoop out most of the soft inside portion of the loaf and save for other purposes, such as stuffing or dried bread crumbs.

In about 2 tablespoons butter, sauté green onions and half the garlic until onions wilt. Do not burn! Cut cream cheese into small chunks and add along with onions, garlic, sour cream, and Cheddar cheese. Mix well. Fold in artichoke hearts.

Put all of this mixture into hollowed out bread. Place top on bread and wrap in a double thickness of heavy-duty aluminum foil.

Bake in 350-degree oven for 1½ to 2 hours.

Slice French rolls thinly and butter with remaining butter and garlic. Wrap in foil and bake with big loaf for the last ½ hour.

When ready, remove foil and serve, using slices of French rolls to dip out sauce. Makes enough for about 10 to 12 as an appetizer.

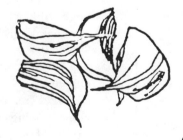

You could wash down the garlic sauce on garlic bread with garlic wine.

LONDON *DAILY MAIL*

35

WOWCHOS

LEONARD BRILL, San Francisco, CA

This spiced-up recipe for nachos with whole baked garlic cloves for extra flavor had the judges rolling their eyes with delight as they awarded second place to its creator.

2	large heads fresh garlic, separated into cloves and peeled
2	tablespoons oil
	Tortilla chips
¼	cup chopped red onion
1	can (4 oz.) chopped green chiles
⅓	cup sliced pimento-stuffed olives (optional)
1½	cups grated Pepper Jack cheese
	Chopped cilantro
	Chopped green onion tops

Coat garlic cloves with oil and bake in 375-degree oven for 30 minutes, or until soft and golden.

Cover metal baking pan (approximately 9 × 12 inches) with overlapping tortilla chips. Distribute garlic, onion, chiles, and olives evenly over the chips.

Cover with cheese and bake at 400 degrees for 5 minutes or until cheese melts. Top with cilantro and green onion and serve.

Makes about 4 appetizer servings.

CREAMY GARLIC SPINACH SOUP WITH GARLIC CROUTONS

DEBRA KAUFMAN, South San Francisco, CA

This soup has fabulous flavor, but be sure to serve it with homemade garlic croutons. Use day-old sourdough French bread if you have it.

Chop spinach coarsely. Combine with chicken broth and carrots in 2- to 3-quart pot. Cook 5 to 10 minutes until carrots are tender and spinach wilted. Remove from heat.

Meanwhile, sauté onion and garlic very gently over low to medium heat in butter, about 20 to 30 minutes. Onions should be very tender and translucent, but garlic should NOT be browned! Add flour and cook, stirring constantly 5 to 10 minutes.

Combine spinach/broth and onion/garlic mixtures in food processor or blender in small batches. Puree until smooth.

Clean pot and return soup to pot. Add cream, whipping cream and salt and freshly ground pepper to taste. Heat until hot, but not boiling.

Garnish with a dollop of sour cream and garlic croutons.

Makes 4 servings.

1	large bunch spinach, stems removed
4	cups chicken broth (preferably homemade)
2	large carrots, grated
1	large onion, chopped
8	cloves fresh garlic, finely chopped
½	cup butter (1 stick)
¼	cup flour
½	cup light cream
½	cup whipping cream
	Salt and freshly ground pepper to taste
	Sour cream (optional)

36

GARLIC CROUTONS:

1	loaf sourdough French bread
¼	cup olive oil
1	teaspoon garlic powder
1	teaspoon crushed dry parsley
¾	teaspoon Hungarian paprika
	Salt and pepper to taste

GARLIC CROUTONS:

Cut bread into 1-inch cubes.

Combine oil with spices and toss with bread cubes.

Spread cubes in shallow baking pan and bake at 325 degrees for about 25 minutes. Store in tightly covered container.

CHICKEN PEPERONATA

STACEY HAROLDSEN, Los Angeles, CA

Though not a winner, this tasty recipe was popular with the judges who thought the combination of garlic, peppers, and balsamic vinegar made a wonderful sauce for the chicken. The fresh basil is an important ingredient also, but if not available dried basil can be substituted.

2	whole chickens, about 3 lbs. *each*
2	tablespoons butter
2	whole heads fresh garlic
	Salt and pepper
2	large sprigs fresh rosemary
3	large green bell peppers
3	large red bell peppers
¼	cup pine nuts
¼	cup extra virgin olive oil
¼	cup Italian balsamic vinegar
1	tablespoon sugar
3	tablespoons chopped fresh basil
	Lettuce leaves and basil sprigs for garnish

Preheat oven to 375 degrees.

Wash chickens and pat dry; rub with butter. Separate cloves of garlic but do not peel. Sprinkle cavities of chickens with salt and pepper; place a sprig of rosemary and half of the garlic cloves in each.

Roast breast-side down for 1 hour, then turn breast-side up and continue roasting until tender, about 15 minutes.

Remove from oven, when cool enough to handle, remove meat from bones, pulling the meat into strips. Reserve cooked garlic cloves.

Broil peppers until skins are charred, then hold under running water while removing skins and seeds. Cut half the peppers into strips and reserve the rest.

Remove skins from 6 of the cooked garlic cloves and mince finely. Toast pine nuts in a dry skillet over medium heat. Combine olive oil, vinegar, and sugar in a bowl. Toss chicken, peppers, pine nuts, basil, minced garlic and dressing. Add salt and pepper to taste.

Line serving platter with lettuce and mound chicken salad on top. Garnish with the reserved peppers, the cooked garlic cloves (skins and all) and basil sprigs. Serve at room temperature.

Makes 6 to 8 servings.

37

PORK AND CHICKEN LOS ARCOS

RAYMOND G. MARSHALL, Pasadena, CA

Some of the ingredients in this recipe may sound a bit exotic, but you'll like the results. The pork and chicken are marinated in advance to give the meat a rich flavor. Canned, peeled lichees are available in most supermarkets or you can substitute chunks of drained, canned pineapple, but it won't taste the same!

3	lbs. pork shoulder
2	lbs. chicken thighs
40	cloves fresh garlic, unpeeled
1	tablespoon salt
1	cup vinegar
2	tablespoons lemon juice
8	bay leaves
½	teaspoon *each* fresh ground pepper and caramel coloring
4	whole cloves
6	very thin slices fresh ginger (*or prepared in light syrup*)
2	tablespoons salad oil
2	tablespoons plain gelatin
2	cans (11 oz. *each*) peeled lichees
1	cup toasted pumpkin seeds

Cut pork into 1½-inch cubes. Bone chicken and cut each thigh into 3 or 4 pieces.

Prepare marinade: Peel, chop, and mash 4 cloves garlic in salt to make a paste. Add vinegar, lemon juice, bay leaves, pepper, caramel coloring, cloves and ginger; mix well.

Pour over pork and chicken and marinate for 6 to 8 hours in the refrigerator, stirring frequently.

Remove pork and chicken from marinade and reserve marinade. Sauté pork in oil for 20 minutes. Add chicken and sauté for another 20 minutes. Then add the remaining 36 cloves unpeeled garlic.

Add gelatin to reserved marinade to soften, adding a little water if necessary. Stir marinade well, add to pork and chicken and cook about 30 minutes or until meat is done and tender.

Add drained lichees and pumpkin seeds to pot. Let cook about 5 minutes to heat through and serve, preferably with steamed rice.

Makes 8 servings.

Note: The garlic cloves are eaten using the fingers to pinch the pulp out of each skin.

38

RABBIT WITH LENTILS

JOHN ROBINSON, Granada Hills, CA

This two-time finalist specializes in hearty dishes made with grains and legumes. In this casserole, rabbit is paired with lentils and finished with the fruity sweetness of apple. An attractive and satisfying meal.

8	rabbit legs and thighs
	Flour, as needed
½	cup butter, unsalted
¼	cup olive oil
1	lb. dried lentils
	Salt and pepper to taste
	Cayenne pepper
½	lb. thick-sliced bacon, cut into 2-inch pieces
20	to 25 cloves fresh garlic, peeled
1½	cups thickly sliced fresh mushrooms
½	cup gin (with strong juniper berry flavor)
½	cup crabapple jelly
½	cup finely chopped parsley
1	can (*or* jar) red spiced crabapples
1	bunch watercress

Dredge rabbit in flour and sauté over moderately high heat in ¼ cup *each* butter and olive oil until brown on all sides. Remove rabbit and save pan with drippings.

Cook lentils according to package instructions, except stop when *slightly* underdone. Drain lentils, stir in remaining ¼ cup butter, and season with salt, pepper, and a generous dash of cayenne pepper.

Line bottom of heavy casserole (with tightly fitting lid) with bacon. Put layer of lentils on top of bacon, add rabbit pieces, heap garlic around rabbit and cover all with balance of lentils. Spread mushrooms on top and seal casserole with aluminum foil.

Then carefully put on the lid and bake at 350 degrees for 1½ hours.

Remove rabbit from casserole and place around edge of serving platter. Stir balance of casserole ingredients together and mount in center of platter.

Heat pan with reserved drippings over moderately high heat, add gin and stir until thoroughly deglazed. Add crabapple jelly and stir until completely combined. Remove from heat, add parsley and stir. Pour over rabbit.

Garnish with crabapples and watercress.

Serves 4.

HOT BRIE PASTA ALA DIANE

DIANE TARANGO, Hacienda Heights, CA

A very simple dish but very, very good. Might need more garlic for some. Be sure the Brie is well ripened, so that it will have good flavor.

1	lb. ripe French Brie
½	cup olive oil
1	cup fresh basil, cut into strips
4	large cloves fresh garlic, minced
4	tomatoes, seeded and cubed
½	teaspoon salt
¾	teaspoon freshly ground pepper
1	lb. linguine *or* capelli d'angelo (angel hair) pasta
6	oz. Parmesan, freshly grated

Remove rind from cheese and cut into irregular pieces. Combine with next 6 ingredients in large bowl and let stand for 2 hours at room temperature.

Cook pasta *al dente* and drain. Toss hot pasta with Brie mixture. Top with Parmesan cheese and serve at once. Delicious!

Makes 4 to 6 servings.

How anything as small and delicate looking as a clove of garlic can have such an impact on food never ceases to amaze.

BETSEY BALSLEY
LOS ANGELES TIMES

GARLIC RAVIOLI

Winner of Prize for Best Recipe Using Most Garlic, 1983
KELLEE KATZMAN, North Hollywood, CA

*For those who like to make their own pasta and who love garlic,
here is an irresistible recipe for ravioli.*

5	large heads fresh garlic
2	cups chicken broth (preferably homemade)
11	tablespoons unsalted butter
1½	cups ricotta cheese
1	cup grated Parmesan cheese
1	teaspoon garlic salt
2	sheets homemade pasta (about 5 × 24 inches *each*)
1	egg, slightly beaten
⅓	cup heavy cream
⅓	cup grated Romano cheese

Put heads of garlic in shallow baking pan; pour chicken broth over and dot each head with 1 tablespoon butter.

Cover and bake for 45 minutes, or until tender.

Strain and reserve ⅓ cup liquid. Allow garlic to cool; then squeeze each clove into a bowl. Discard skins. Add ricotta, ½ cup Parmesan, and garlic salt and mix thoroughly.

Brush 1 sheet of pasta with egg and place garlic-cheese mixture on pasta in mounds (1 teaspoon each) about 2 inches apart.

Place second sheet of pasta over the first and press with fingers around each mound. With fluted pastry wheel, cut up into 2-inch square ravioli. Refrigerate for 30 minutes.

Bring large pot of water to boil. Just before water boils, start sauce.

In frying pan, melt remaining 6 tablespoons butter, add cream and reduce slightly. Add reserved ⅓ cup liquid and reduce to good sauce consistency.

When water reaches a rapid boil, drop ravioli in and boil for 3 to 5 minutes. Remove with slotted spoon and put directly into reduced sauce. Sprinkle with remaining Parmesan and Romano cheeses.

Serves 4 to 6 as an appetizer.

41

MAHONY'S BRUSCHETTA

Winner of 1983 Recipe Contest
NEIL MAHONY, Ventura, CA

This recipe is one of the all-time favorite prizewinners. An unusual and outstanding dish. The Mahonys recommend keeping a bottle of olive oil in the refrigerator to which have been added four to five heads of peeled garlic. That way you'll have it ready when you want to make bruschetta or you can add lemon juice for a salad dressing, to prepare oysters and linguine or to add to pasta water for flavor and to prevent boilover.

1	loaf French *or* Italian bread without seeds (day-old bread works fine)
10	large cloves fresh garlic, peeled
¾	cup olive oil, preferably extra virgin
1½	cups whipping cream
½	cup grated Locatelli cheese (hard Romano cheese)
½	cup grated Parmesan cheese, preferably imported Italian
3	tablespoons butter
1	tablespoon chopped parsley
	Paprika

Cut bread diagonally in 1-inch slices, without cutting through bottom crust.

In food processor or blender, chop garlic fine with steel blade and add olive oil with processor running to make a thin paste. Slather garlic paste on cut surfaces and on top and side crusts of bread.

Place in 350-degree oven, directly on rack (with pan on shelf below to catch drippings), and bake for 10 to 12 minutes, until top is crispy looking.

While bread is in oven, heat whipping cream in heavy saucepan. Do not boil. Stir in cheeses slowly so that sauce is absolutely smooth (a wire whip works well for this). Stir in butter and keep sauce warm until bread is ready.

Wait until everyone is seated at the table. Then place crispy bread in a warmed, shallow serving dish with sides. Finish cutting through bottom crust and pour sauce over. Sprinkle with parsley and paprika and serve IMMEDI-ATELY. This dish cools very quickly.

Makes 6 servings.

Note: Each guest should be provided with a small saucer for the bruschetta, as it is best eaten with a knife and fork.

42

GARLIC PANCAKES WITH HAM SAUCE

JOHN KEITH DRUMMOND, San Francisco, CA

Cooking the garlic until it is soft changes its flavor from pungent to sweet and nutlike— a very good addition to pancakes and a pleasant complement to the smokiness of the ham sauce. Serve for breakfast, brunch, lunch or even a light supper.

Mix together 12 tablespoons (1½ sticks) butter and sage; reserve.

Remove as much outer skin from garlic as possible without piercing the cloves' covering. Set garlic in saucepan, cover with water and boil gently about 45 minutes or until cloves are quite soft. Remove from heat.

When cool enough to handle squeeze each clove to remove cooked garlic by grasping clove at the tip and pulling down toward base. In mixing bowl, beat garlic with fork until smooth. You should have about 1 cup of garlic. Add to garlic about same amount (at least 1 cup) flour, eggs, oil and 1½ cups milk to make pancake batter. Add minced garlic to batter and set aside.

Melt remaining 4 tablespoons butter and keep warm. While waiting for batter to work, place half the sage butter (6 tablespoons) in saucepan, add 6 tablespoons flour to make a roux and cook at medium temperature, stirring frequently, to brown.

Meanwhile in skillet, place 2 tablespoons of remaining sage butter and add ham. Heat through, but do not burn. When roux is nicely browned, add remaining 2 cups milk. Allow to thicken, stirring frequently. Add ham and skillet drippings and mix to make ham sauce. Keep warm.

Heat griddle or clean skillet and grease lightly with a bit of remaining sage butter. Drop batter by spoonfuls onto griddle to make silver dollar-size pancakes. Serve with melted butter and ham sauce.

Makes 2 dozen pancakes.

½	lb. butter
3	tablespoons rubbed sage
3	large heads fresh garlic
2	cups self-rising flour, approx.
2	eggs
2	tablespoons oil
3½	cups milk
9	large cloves fresh garlic, minced
1	lb. lean ham, minced

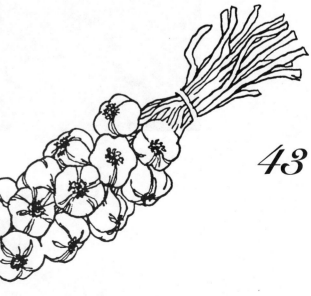

43

1984

*N*ervously, Epstein eyed her competitors.
"Omigod," she said.
"These are heavy-duty garlic freaks."

OAKLAND *TRIBUNE*

OYSTERS GILROY

JUDGE STEVEN E. HALPERN, Emeryville, CA

The unusual aniselike flavor of the Pernod used in this recipe helps to create a sauce of intriguing complexity which blends very well with the oysters. An excellent first course for a very special dinner.

12	medium cloves fresh garlic, unpeeled
½	ripe avocado
¾	teaspoon salt
⅛	teaspoon black pepper
1/16	teaspoon cayenne pepper
3	tablespoons Pernod
2	tablespoons Worcestershire sauce
2	tablespoons heavy cream
4	tablespoons melted butter
2	dozen medium-size oysters in half shell
	Rock salt

Wrap garlic in aluminum foil and bake in 325-degree oven for ½ hour. Cool to room temperature.

Pinch cloves and squeeze out garlic. Add to food processor with remaining ingredients except butter and oysters and process until mixture is thoroughly pureed. Then add butter in slow stream until incorporated into puree.

Place oysters in half shell on bed of rock salt in baking pan. Bake at 450 degrees on middle level of oven for 6 minutes. Remove.

Cover each oyster with puree and return to oven for 1 minute.

Serve with sourdough bread and dry white wine.

Makes 4 to 6 appetizer servings.

45

BAKED STUFFED GARLIC CLAMS

ROSINA WILSON, Albany, CA

This marvelous hors d'oeuvre is festive, elegant, and absolutely a snap to prepare. Serve with a dry California or Italian white wine such as Sauvignon Blanc or Soave. Or serve champagne to heighten the mood of the festivity.

20	to 30 cloves fresh garlic
3	cans (6½ oz. *each*) chopped clams, drained (about 1½ cups) or the equivalent in steamed, chopped fresh clams
¾	cup butter, softened
1	tablespoon fresh oregano *or* 1 teaspoon dried
⅓	cup frozen *or* fresh cooked spinach
¼	cup sherry
1	cup French bread crumbs
¼	cup minced parsley
2	tablespoons lemon juice
2	teaspoons pignoli (pine nuts) *or* chopped walnuts
½	teaspoon salt
¼	teaspoon *each* nutmeg, black pepper, and cayenne pepper

GARNISHES:

Sliced large fresh garlic cloves dipped in olive oil, pignoli, cayenne pepper and lemon wedges

Mince or press garlic to make ¾ cup.

In large bowl, mix garlic and other ingredients, except garnishes, and spoon generously into clam or scallop shells. Decorate each with a slice of garlic, pignoli and sprinkle of cayenne pepper.

Bake at 375 degrees for 25 to 30 minutes until bread crumbs turn golden brown and centers are cooked through. Serve piping hot with lemon wedges.

Makes about 8 servings.

There's something about garlic that creates excitement. People can get real loose around garlic.

LLOYD HARRIS
TIME MAGAZINE

APPETIZER GARLIC PUFFS

ROXANNE CHAN, Albany, CA

*The garlic filling used to make this appetizer can also be used to stuff
cold cooked artichokes and cold, blanched green peppers
or as a topping for cold sliced meats.*

1	**small head fresh garlic, separated into cloves**
	Boiling water
½	**cup butter**
1	**cup all-purpose flour**
¼	**teaspoon salt**
4	**eggs**

GARLIC FILLING:

1	**small head fresh garlic, separated into cloves**
	Boiling water
2	**cups whipped cream (about ½ pint)**
1	**cup grated Parmesan cheese**
1	**green onion, finely chopped**
2	**tablespoons *each* chopped pimento, black olives, and roasted almonds**

Cover garlic cloves with boiling water. Let stand 5 minutes. Drain and peel. Finely mince.

In a saucepan, melt butter in 1 cup boiling water. Add garlic, flour, and salt all at once. Cook, stirring, until mixture forms a ball. Remove from heat.

Cool slightly, then add eggs one at a time, beating after each addition until mixture is smooth.

Drop by teaspoonfuls on a greased baking sheet. Bake in a 400-degree oven for 10 minutes. Reduce heat to 325 degrees and continue to cook for 20 to 25 minutes or until golden.

Remove from oven and cut in half. Cool. Fill with Garlic Filling.

Makes about 20 appetizer puffs.

FILLING:

Cover garlic cloves with boiling water. Cook until cloves are soft. Peel and mash.

Stir mashed garlic into whipped cream along with remaining ingredients.

APHRA DE JACQUES
KATHE HEWITT, La Jolla, CA

This prize-winning cook named her recipe to approximate the word "aphrodisiac," because her husband claimed eating it made him amorous. Who knows! Legend attributes garlic with many such tantalizing properties and this dish certainly cast a spell on the judges!

1½ lb.	Monterey Jack cheese (7 × 3-inch block)
30	cloves fresh garlic
4	cups peanut oil (more as needed)
1	tablespoon Italian seasoning
3	eggs, beaten
2	cups all-purpose flour
3	cups French bread crumbs*
3	tablespoons chopped fresh parsley
1	small jar marinara sauce

FRIED JACK HORS D'OEUVRES:

Slice cheese into 30 slices about ¼ inch thick.

Peel garlic and slice each clove lengthwise into about 6 ovals.

Heat oil in deep, heavy saucepan over medium-low heat. Add garlic ovals and simmer 5 to 7 minutes, being careful not to burn or brown them. Remove slices as they float to surface and are light brown in color. Drain on paper towel. Reserve oil for cheese.

Mince garlic and mix with Italian seasoning.

Spread half the cheese slices evenly with garlic mixture. Press remaining cheese slices on each to make 15 bars.

Dip flour-coated pieces into egg again, then into bread crumbs mixed with parsley. Be sure to cover sides.

Reheat oil to medium-high and fry cheese in oil a few pieces at a time until lightly browned (takes about 2 minutes). Skim particles from oil as they accumulate.

Drain cheese on paper towels and keep warm until all are fried.

Serve with toothpicks and Marina Sauce for dipping. Makes about 15 pieces.

Note: Use day-old bread and prepare crumbs in food processor. Dry packaged crumbs may be used but are not as attractive when fried.

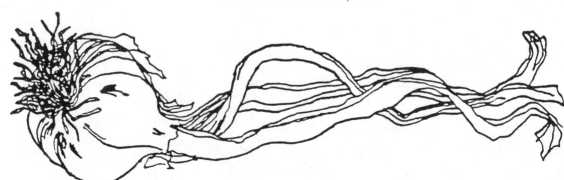

WHOLE GARLIC APPETIZER
PATRICK MARKEY, Los Angeles, CA

*Our garlic appetizer can be held in the refrigerator for up to 10 days.
It's especially good for those who enjoy snacking
on tart and tangy tidbits.*

½	cup olive oil
8	whole heads fresh garlic
2	large sweet red onions, quartered
1	tablespoon whole peppercorns
4	stalks celery, chopped
4	medium carrots, sliced
¼	teaspoon *each* rosemary, thyme, oregano, marjoram, coriander, basil (fresh if possible)
¾	cup white wine vinegar
¼	cup dry white wine
½	cup water
8	to 10 bay leaves
½	teaspoon dry mustard
1	small can pickled green chiles, about 4 oz.

Heat oil in skillet.

Peel outer covering from garlic heads and take a ½-inch slice from top of each head, exposing meat of cloves, but leaving heads intact.

Sauté garlic, onions, and peppercorns in oil for 3 minutes.

Add celery, carrots, rosemary, thyme, oregano, marjoram, coriander, and basil. Sauté 5 minutes, stirring.

Add vinegar, wine, water, bay leaves and dry mustard. Simmer for 10 minutes.

Stir in chiles and simmer for 3 minutes.

Remove from heat, strain, reserving garlic and 1 cup cooking liquid. Place garlic heads in flat baking dish. Pour reserved liquid over, cover and refrigerate.

Serve cold as an appetizer for spreading on French bread rounds or crackers. Also can be eaten plain as a relish course or cloves peeled and mixed in salads.

Makes 8 servings.

PEANUTS AND SLIVERS
FERNANDA S. DE LUNA, Daly City, CA

*Here is one snack or party treat that will disappear faster than you can
refill the bowl. Or you may just be too selfish to share them with others.
A true taste sensation for the serious garlic-holic!*

Place peanuts in wok that has been preheated with oil to medium-high. Make sure there is enough oil in wok to cover peanuts. Stir peanuts constantly, being careful not to burn them. As peanuts begin to brown slightly, lower heat to simmer, continuing to stir, and cook until light golden brown.

Drain peanuts well in wire basket and let cool.

Place garlic in skillet preheated with 1½ cups vegetable oil until it reaches medium-high. Stir garlic constantly to attain a consistent color and to prevent burning or sticking of garlic. As garlic browns slightly, reduce heat to low and continue to stir and cook until garlic is crisp and light golden brown. Drain garlic in the same manner as peanuts, breaking up any clusters. Cool.

Combine peanuts and garlic and salt to taste. Store in airtight containers until ready to devour!

2	lbs. peanuts, raw, shelled and skinned, about 6 cups (available in health food and nut stores)
6	whole heads fresh garlic, peeled and sliced to make about 2½ cups slivered garlic
	Vegetable oil for frying peanuts and garlic separately
	Salt to taste

49

SPICY GARLIC CHICKEN

CINDY NEVA, Acton, CA

Yum. Yum. This dish is good and spicy and at its best when the chicken is allowed to marinate overnight in the refrigerator.

1	bunch cilantro *with* roots
1	large whole head fresh garlic, peeled
2	tablespoons coarse black pepper
1	teaspoon ground curry powder
¼	teaspoon crushed red chile pepper
¼	cup peanut oil
⅓	cup soy sauce
1	whole chicken *or* 12 drumsticks, wings *or* thighs
	Sweet Garlic Sauce for Dipping (recipe below)

SWEET GARLIC SAUCE FOR DIPPING:

3	cups sugar
1	cup vinegar
2	tablespoons coarse black pepper
1	teaspoon dry red chile pepper
½	teaspoon salt
1	drop red food coloring
1	whole head fresh garlic, peeled and chopped

Cut roots off cilantro and place with garlic, some cilantro leaves and a few stems in food processor and whirl until coarsely chopped, or chop by hand.

Turn mixture into bowl, add remaining whole cilantro leaves, pepper, curry powder, chile pepper, peanut oil, and soy sauce. Mix well.

Pour mixture over chicken and marinate 4 hours or as long as overnight.

Meanwhile prepare Sweet Garlic Sauce for Dipping.

Barbecue chicken over low glowing coals about 1 hour, basting occasionally and turning chicken several times.

Serve with Sweet Garlic Sauce for Dipping. Makes 4 servings.

SAUCE:

In 2-quart saucepan bring sugar and vinegar to boil.

Add pepper, chile pepper, salt and food coloring. Boil 5 minutes, stirring to prevent sticking. (Be careful not to permit mixture to boil over pan.)

Remove from heat and stir in chopped garlic. Refrigerate.

50

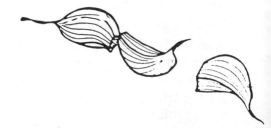

ROASTED GARLIC PUREE DIP

Winner Best Recipe Using Most Garlic, 1984
MARY FENCL, Forestdale, MA

This is a truly versatile recipe. The puree can be used on cooked vegetables, fish, steaks, salad greens or baked potatoes. You can double the recipe if you want to keep some on hand.

6	large heads fresh garlic (about 72 cloves)
2	pkgs. (8 oz. *each*) cream cheese, at room temperature
4	oz. blue cheese, at room temperature
¾	cup milk
2	tablespoons chopped fresh parsley
	Crudités (mixed fresh vegetables, sliced for dipping)

Remove outer covering on garlic. Do not peel or separate the cloves. Place each garlic head on a large square of heavy aluminum foil. Fold up the foil, so the cloves are completely wrapped.

Bake for 1 hour at 350 degrees.

Remove garlic from oven and cool for 10 minutes. Separate cloves and squeeze cloves to remove cooked garlic. Discard skins.

In food processor, mix cheeses, milk and garlic until smooth.

Place in serving dish. Sprinkle with parsley. Serve with crudités for dipping.

Makes about 5 cups.

CALIFORNIA CHICKEN

JAN E. SHELTON, Escondido, CA

In this recipe chicken breasts are browned in butter and then baked covered with a garlic cream sauce. When done they are beautifully presented garnished with colorful slices of California avocado and mandarin oranges.

60	cloves fresh garlic (about 5 heads)
	Boiling water
3	cups whipping cream
	Salt and white pepper to taste
¼	cup butter
4	whole chicken breasts, split, skinned, and boned
⅛	teaspoon *each* cinnamon and dried tarragon
2	ripe avocados
	Juice of 1 lime
1	small can (6 oz.) mandarin orange slices, drained
1	tablespoon chopped fresh parsley
	Paprika

Place garlic cloves in a saucepan with boiling water to cover. Boil for 2 minutes. Drain, then peel cloves.

Return garlic to pan and add whipping cream. Simmer, stirring occasionally, until garlic is very tender and cream is thickened and reduced by half.

Rub garlic and cream through a wire sieve. Return to saucepan and season with salt and pepper. Set aside and place plastic wrap on cream surface.

Heat butter in frying pan over medium-high heat. Add chicken and sauté for 1 minute, turning chicken once. Do not brown.

Place chicken on oven-proof platter. Bake in 325-degree oven 7 to 10 minutes.

Meanwhile peel avocados, cut into ½-inch slices and toss with lime juice.

Pour garlic mixture over chicken and return to oven for 2 or 3 minutes.

Garnish with drained avocado and orange slices. Sprinkle with chopped fresh parsley and paprika to taste. Serve at once.

Makes 4 to 6 servings.

51

GRILLED FISH WITH GARLIC SALSA

Winner of 1984 Recipe Contest
BEVERLY STONE, Berkeley, CA

"To win first prize, improvise," said Beverly Stone, and improvise she did. Her recipe was developed out of necessity when she found herself with only a few ingredients in the house which, when combined became an outstanding new garlic salsa to serve over fish. The judges agreed it was quite a catch.

Mix together olive oil, 4 tablespoons lemon juice, slivered garlic, ¼ cup chopped cilantro, and salt and pepper to taste.

Add fish fillets and marinate for 1 hour or as long as overnight.

Meanwhile prepare Garlic Salsa. In a frying pan over medium heat, melt 2 tablespoons butter. Sauté onion, chiles, and minced garlic until soft, stirring. Add tomatoes and the remaining 1 tablespoon lemon juice. Cook, stirring, for 10 minutes. Remove from heat and add salt and pepper to taste. Stir in remaining ⅓ cup chopped cilantro. Slowly stir in remaining butter until melted.

Barbecue fish over low glowing coals about 7 minutes or until done to your liking, turning fish once. Remove to warm serving platter.

Top with Garlic Salsa. Garnish with lemon wedges and reserved cilantro leaves. Makes 6 servings.

Note: Angler (sometimes called monkfish) is particularly good in this recipe.

½	cup fruity olive oil
5	tablespoons lemon juice
4	cloves fresh garlic, peeled and slivered
1	bunch fresh cilantro, chopped to make ½ cup, (reserve some whole leaves for garnish)
	Salt and freshly ground pepper to taste
6	firm-fleshed fish fillets, about 6 oz. each and ¾ inch thick*
¼	lb. sweet butter
¼	cup chopped sweet red onion
2	small hot green chiles, finely minced
1	tablespoon finely minced fresh garlic
1	lb. ripe tomatoes, peeled and chopped
	Lemon wedges

52

SPAGHETTACCINI CAROLINI

ROBERT J. DYER, Gilroy, CA

"If you live in the Garlic Capital of the World, it's only fitting that you should be a good garlic cook," claims Bob Dyer, Gilroy businessman, who was also chairman of the very first Garlic Festival in 1979. Bob's colorful spaghetti dish attracted the judges with its stir-fried vegetables, succulent prawns and plenty of garlic—24 cloves in all.

1	lb. spaghetti noodles
4	tablespoons oil
¼	lb. butter
24	cloves fresh garlic, peeled and chopped
1	lb. fresh jumbo shrimp, peeled and butterflied
1	red bell pepper, thinly sliced
1	bunch broccoli, cut into serving-size spears
2	cups chopped fresh mushrooms
1	cup chopped fresh parsley
1	cup chopped green onions
1	tablespoon dried red pepper
2	tablespoons flour
½	cup dry white wine
1	pint heavy cream
1	small wedge (about 3 oz.) Parmesan cheese, grated
	Salt to taste

Cook noodles according to package directions in boiling water with 2 tablespoons oil.

Meanwhile, melt butter in large skillet over medium, high heat. Add chopped garlic and shrimp; cook until shrimp turn pink, but do not allow garlic to brown. Set aside.

In another skillet, over medium-high heat, stir-fry red bell pepper and broccoli in remaining 2 tablespoons oil. Cook until crisp-tender. Drain and set aside.

Add mushrooms, half the parsley, onions and dried red pepper to garlic and shrimp; sauté for 1 minute.

Add flour, mix thoroughly, and add wine. Simmer for about 30 seconds, then add cream and heat through, stirring.

Drain noodles and add to sauce with half the grated cheese. Toss gently until noodles are well coated and cheese is melted. Salt lightly.

If sauce is too thin, continue heating until sauce reduces to a creamy consistency. If sauce is too thick, add cream.

Gently toss in the stir-fried vegetables.

Garnish with remaining chopped parsley and grated cheese and serve immediately.

Makes 8 servings.

53

1985

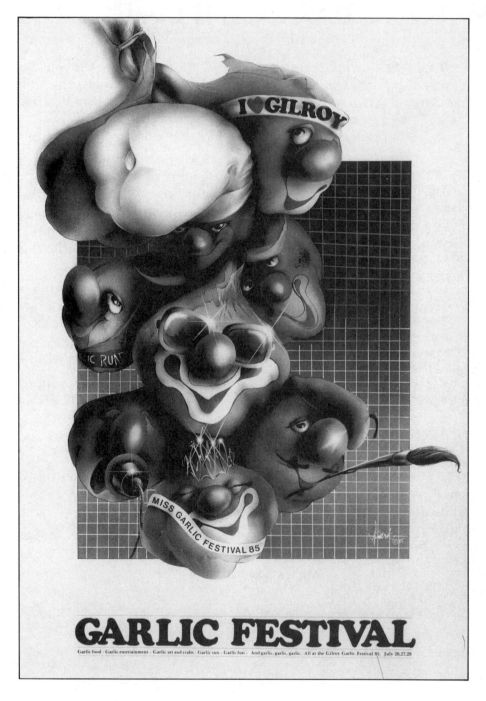

Garlic: from Dracula to pasta, herb reeks of history.

C.C.U. GARLIC-STUFFED JALAPEÑOS
BECKY BOEHME, Portland, OR

Here's another one for the stouthearted. As a matter of fact, Becky made up this appetizer when she was working in the coronary care unit of an Oregon hospital.

Blend avocado and cream cheese with a fork. Add garlic, onion and bell pepper. Mix thoroughly.

Trim stems from jalapeño peppers. Cut in halves lengthwise. Remove seeds. Fill each half with approximately 1 tablespoon of filling.

Serve either at room temperature or chilled. Filling may be stored in refrigerator for up to 5 days.

Makes 40 to 60 stuffed jalapeños.

1	large ripe avocado, peeled and mashed
1	pkg. (8 oz.) cream cheese, softened
2	whole heads fresh garlic, finely chopped
1	large yellow onion, finely chopped
⅓	to ½ large bell pepper, finely chopped
20	to 30 jalapeño peppers, canned in oil

LADY SINGS THE GREENS
DEBBIE SHEESLEY, Sacramento, CA

No one will be singing the blues when you serve this stepped-up version of the ubiquitous tossed green salad. The secret's in the dressing.

4	large egg yolks
2	tablespoons Dijon-style mustard
¼	cup minced cilantro
¼	cup bacon, cooked crisp, drained and crumbled into small bits
6	cloves fresh garlic, minced
1	cup virgin olive oil
⅓	cup red wine vinegar
	Salt and pepper to taste
1	bunch spinach
1	head endive
1	head butter lettuce
1	English cucumber, thinly sliced
2	or 3 hard-cooked eggs, yolks crumbled, whites shaved
	Parmesan cheese, grated
	Garlic croutons

In a blender or food processor, whirl egg yolks and mustard until smooth and pale yellow in color. Whirl in cilantro, bacon, and garlic.

Alternately add oil and vinegar, drop by drop, until well blended. Adjust flavor with salt and pepper.

Wash spinach, remove stems and pat dry. Separate endive and butter lettuce leaves, wash and pat dry.

Tear greens into medium-size pieces and place in large salad bowl. Toss with enough dressing to coat.

Portion out onto individual chilled salad plates. Sprinkle with Parmesan cheese. Garnish with cucumber slices, egg yolks and whites, and croutons.

Makes 6 servings.

55

JOYCIE-A'S CHICKEN PROVINCIAL

JOYCE A. BROWER, San Diego, CA

The combined flavors of garlic and thyme permeate the chicken in this marvelous one-dish meal.

1	whole head fresh garlic
1	chicken, cut into quarters
4	potatoes, peeled
3	carrots, sliced diagonally
2	onions, quartered
20	cherry tomatoes
20	mushrooms
1	cup pitted ripe olives, drained
1	cup olive oil
1	tablespoon dried thyme
	Salt and pepper to taste

Break garlic into cloves, peel and cut into slivers. Place garlic under the skin of the chicken and in holes which have been poked into the chicken. Use entire head of garlic.

Place chicken in roasting pan, add potatoes, carrots, onions, tomatoes, mushrooms and olives. Pour olive oil over all and sprinkle heavily with thyme, until chicken is nearly green in color.

Bake, uncovered, 1½ hours at 350 degrees. Baste every 15 minutes.

Serve with French bread to soak up the wonderful juices.

DR. JENSEN'S UNCENSORED 7-CLOVE HASH

DR. CARL JENSEN, Cotati, CA

According to Dr. Jensen, this hash was created for First Amendment garlic aficionados. It originated with his Danish father, and is called "uncensored" because "no sensitive or controversial ingredients should be left out of a true hash.... Everything in the kitchen is fair game."

7	cloves fresh garlic, minced
½	cup diced red onion
⅓	cup diced celery
⅓	cup diced green pepper
⅓	cup diced mushrooms
⅓	cup chopped scallions
2	cups diced roast beef
1	cup diced cooked potatoes
	Seasonings to taste: salt, pepper, basil, oregano, parsley, crushed red pepper, garlic powder, Worcestershire sauce, hot green chile salsa, Burgundy and Tabasco (sparingly)
4	extra-large eggs

In a large well-greased skillet, combine garlic, red onion, celery, green pepper, mushrooms, and scallions and sauté slowly and lovingly over medium heat.

When golden brown, mix in meat and potatoes, raising heat to medium high. Cook until a crust starts to form on bottom, then stir constantly to let hash brown throughout while adding seasonings to taste.

When nearly browned throughout, pat mixture down firmly to form a level cake.

Carve out four evenly-spaced holes. Crack and slip an egg into each of the holes, being careful not to break the yolks.

Turn heat back to medium and be patient. Serve on warmed plates when the egg whites are firm but the yolks still soft.

Makes 4 terrific servings.

GARLIC-STUFFED LEG OF LAMB WITH CABERNET SAUCE

BARBARA WAYMIRE, assisted by TIM LAVALLI, Manhattan Beach, CA

In this dish, the leg of lamb is stuffed with a puree made with eight heads of garlic, fresh rosemary, and anchovy paste. For best results, use a good drinkable cabernet to marinate the meat, as the wine will later be reduced to sauce the meat.

1	leg of lamb, about 5 to 6 lbs., boned
2	to 3 cups cabernet sauvignon
6	to 8 large heads fresh garlic, broken into cloves, unpeeled
1½	tablespoons finely minced fresh rosemary
1½	teaspoons anchovy paste
3	bunches fresh spinach (about 5 to 6 cups tightly packed)
1	to 2 teaspoons arrowroot
1	tablespoon whole fresh rosemary leaves, stripped from stem

Remove excess fat and skin from outside of lamb. Lay meat flat with boned-out side up. Make deep gashes in thick areas of the meat so that it is of consistent height and thickness. These gashes will also provide pockets for the stuffing, and meat will cook evenly.

Place meat in a deep bowl and pour enough wine over to almost cover. Marinate for 1 to 2 hours.

Place garlic in saucepan and cover with water. Simmer 10 minutes until cloves are soft. Do not overcook! Drain and rinse with cold water. Cut off stem end, pinch at bottom and pop cloves out. Mash garlic into a thick paste or process in blender. Add minced rosemary and anchovy paste and blend well.

Remove meat from marinade, reserving marinade liquid. Lay meat flat with uncut side down and spread paste evenly over inside and down into pockets.

Wash spinach; remove stems and coarse ribs. Place in a nonstick pan and, using only the water left clinging to the leaves after washing, cook over high heat, covered, for 1 minute. Turn as necessary to evenly wilt spinach. Remove excess water by squeezing.

Distribute spinach evenly over paste-covered meat surface. Roll lamb into roast form and truss with twine in 1-inch pattern. Spread excess garlic mixture that may ooze out during trussing over exterior of finished rolled meat.

Roast in preheated 500-degree oven for 10 minutes to sear outside of lamb. Reduce to 325 degrees for 10 minutes per pound. Allow lamb to "set up" for 15 minutes before carving.

SAUCE:

Meanwhile, place marinade in saucepan and heat over medium heat until sauce is reduced by half. Skim if necessary. Thicken with arrowroot which has been dissolved in cold water. Add whole fresh rosemary leaves, reheat and serve with sliced lamb.

Makes 10 to 12 servings.

57

RENEE'S SEAFOOD FRA DIAVOLO

Winner of 1985 Recipe Contest
RENEE N. TELESE, Saugus, CA

The base for the sauce in this dish is a puree of mushrooms, onions, red peppers, mint, basil, oregano and, of course, garlic—½ cup of it. Try this seafood pasta casserole and you'll know why it took first prize in the '85 Cook-off.

½	cup chopped fresh garlic
¼	cup olive oil
1	small lobster in the shell (about 1 lb.), cleaned, small claws and antennae removed
6	large shrimp, cleaned and deveined
¼	lb. fresh mushrooms, sliced
1	small onion, chopped
5	leaves *each* fresh mint, fresh basil and fresh oregano, chopped
¼ to ½	teaspoon crushed dried red pepper
1	teaspoon clam *or* chicken soup base (paste *or* granulated)
1	cup dry white *or* red wine
1	can (28 oz.) whole Italian tomatoes with basil, including juice
8	large mussels, scrubbed
8	large clams, scrubbed
¼	cup chopped fresh parsley
1	lb. thin spaghetti *or* vermicelli, cooked and drained

In 14-inch skillet, cook ¼ cup garlic in hot oil over high heat for 2 to 3 minutes, being careful not to burn.

Add lobster and shrimp to skillet and cook on high heat for 3 to 4 minutes, until lobster turns pink. Remove lobster and shrimp and set aside.

Add remaining ¼ cup garlic, mushrooms, onion, mint, basil, oregano, and red pepper. Cook over medium heat 7 to 9 minutes, stirring frequently.

Pour mixture from skillet into blender or food processor. Add clam or chicken soup base, wine and tomatoes and puree.

Pour puree into 2- to 3-quart saucepan and cook over medium-high heat, adding mussels and clams when mixture begins to boil. Stir often until mussels and clams open, then add parsley.

Remove clams and mussels to dish with lobster and shrimp.

Toss pasta with 2 cups of sauce and line bottom of large ovenproof serving platter with coated pasta. Place lobster in center on top of pasta and place shrimp, mussels and clams decoratively on both sides. Pour remaining sauce over the top, being careful not to hide the shellfish.

Cover with foil and place in preheated 375-degree oven for 7 to 10 minutes. Serve when piping hot.

Makes 4 to 6 servings.

58

SICILIAN GARLIC ROLL

ROXANNE E. CHAN, Albany, CA

A real mediterranean treat…perfect as a first course or as part of a buffet.

SAUCE:

4	tomatoes, peeled, seeded and chopped
⅓	cup olive oil
¼	cup chopped fresh basil leaves
4	cloves fresh garlic, peeled and finely minced
1	tablespoon balsamic vinegar

ROLL:

2	large heads fresh garlic, separated into unpeeled cloves
	Boiling water
2	cups ricotta cheese
1	raw egg
½	cup currants
4	sheets phyllo dough, covered with damp towel to prevent drying out
¼	cup melted butter
½	cup toasted pine nuts

In bowl, combine all sauce ingredients and set aside to blend flavors.

Cover unpeeled garlic cloves with boiling water and cook until cloves are soft. Peel and mash.

Combine garlic with ricotta and egg; mix well. Stir in currants.

Place 1 sheet of phyllo dough on a damp cloth. Brush with butter. Place a second sheet over the first and brush with butter. Repeat with 2 additional sheets.

Spread ricotta mixture over the top sheet. Top with pine nuts. Lift towel gently away from you to form a roll. Pick up towel and put roll on a buttered baking sheet.

Prick in several places and bake at 350 degrees for 35 minutes or until the roll is golden. Cool.

Place sauce in small glass bowl and put in center of platter. Slice roll and arrange attractively around bowl.

Makes 6 servings.

Garlic is a habit and a passion.

KIM UPTON
CHICAGO *SUN-TIMES*

1986

GILROY

GARLIC

FESTIVAL

JULY 25, 26, 27 1986

*Three nickels will get you on the subway,
but garlic will get you a seat.*

NEW YORK YIDDISH SAYING

CREAM OF ROASTED GARLIC SOUP

PATTY FILICE, Gilroy, CA

Some of the best garlic recipes come right from Gilroy. Here's one—a rich, filling soup that would go well with a light seafood or poultry entree.

2	medium-sized heads fresh garlic
	Olive oil
½	cup finely chopped onion
2	tablespoons unsalted butter
1½	cups buttermilk
½	cup cream
1	to 2 small potatoes, baked, skins removed
2	tablespoons cognac
⅛	teaspoon fresh dill
	Salt to taste
	Sourdough French bread cubes, several days old, sautéed in butter and garlic

Place garlic heads on cookie sheet, sprinkle with olive oil and bake in 350-degree oven for 1 hour. Let cool. Cut off end of each clove and squeeze out contents. (Garlic will be soft and creamy.) Set aside.

Sauté chopped onion in butter until softened. Add buttermilk and cream and simmer for 5 minutes. Pour mixture into a food processor.

Rice potato and add with garlic to onion and buttermilk mixture. Puree until smooth.

Return mixture to sauté pan. Add cognac, dill, and salt. Heat thoroughly.

If soup is too thin, add additional potato. If soup is too thick, add additional buttermilk. Serve immediately, garnished with additional dill and croutons.

Makes 4 servings.

GARLICKY TOMATO SAFFRON SOUP

ELLEN SZITA, San Francisco, CA

This soup will bring raves whether it is served hot, cold, or at room temperature.

Place canned chicken broth in freezer so fat will rise to surface for easy removal.

Bring water to boil. Add saffron threads and let steep, uncovered, off heat.

Skin tomatoes by putting them in boiling water for 1 minute. Seed and chop tomatoes.

Chop leeks fine. Heat olive oil in soup pot over medium heat. Do not let oil smoke. Add chopped leeks and sauté just until limp but not brown. When leeks are limp, squeeze garlic cloves through press into leeks and mix over medium heat for 2 minutes. Remove from heat.

Remove chicken broth from freezer and remove fat clumped at the top. Add chicken broth, saffron water including threads, tomatoes, thyme, and fennel to leeks in soup pot.

Simmer mixture, partially covered, for 30 minutes. Five minutes before soup is ready, add spinach.

Serve hot, room temperature, or cold with hearty, crusty bread. Makes 4 to 6 servings.

6	cans (10½ oz. *each*) chicken broth
1	cup boiling water
¼	gram Spanish saffron threads
1	lb. Roma tomatoes, skinned, seeded and chopped in bite-size pieces
1	bunch (3 medium or 1½ cups) leeks, white part only, cleaned
4	tablespoons virgin olive oil
5	large cloves fresh garlic
½	teaspoon dried thyme
6	whole fennel seeds
8	large fresh spinach leaves

61

SUSIE TOWNSEND'S EX-HUSBAND'S SESAME BROCCOLI PASTA SALAD SIGNIFICANTLY IMPROVED

SUSIE TOWNSEND, New York, NY

With a name like this, there's no need for further description.

1	large bunch broccoli, trimmed and broken into florets
3	tablespoons soy sauce
6	cloves fresh garlic, *or* more to your taste, minced
4	tablespoons hot sesame oil (*or* 2 tablespoons chili oil and 2 tablespoons sesame oil)
3	tablespoons white vinegar
2	teaspoons honey
½	cup sesame seeds, toasted in a dry skillet
⅓	cup pine nuts, toasted in a dry skillet
1	bunch scallions, chopped
1	medium red onion, sliced thin
1	lb. fusilli (corkscrew pasta), cooked

Steam broccoli 2 to 3 minutes until tender but still crisp.

In bottom of large salad bowl, combine soy sauce, garlic, oil, vinegar, and honey to make dressing.

Add ¼ cup sesame seeds, pine nuts, scallions, and red onion. Mix well. Then add pasta and toss until well coated. Add broccoli and toss again. Then sprinkle on remaining sesame seeds.

(The salad is best only slightly chilled, better the next day. If refrigerated overnight, let it come almost to room temperature before serving.)

Makes 6 to 8 servings.

62

MARINATED EGGPLANT

BETTY WENGER, Gilroy, CA

Keep a batch in the refrigerator and you'll always be ready when unexpected guests drop by.

2	eggplants
	Salt
5	cups wine vinegar
30	cloves fresh garlic, chopped
3	tablespoons oregano
1½	cups oil

Peel and slice eggplants. Lay slices on board and sprinkle generously with salt. Put another board on top and leave overnight.

In large pot, bring wine vinegar to a boil. Put 4 to 5 pieces of eggplant in deep fry basket: submerge in vinegar and boil 3 to 4 minutes. Remove and pat dry on towel.

In baking dish with lid, layer eggplant slices, garlic, oregano, and oil in several layers until all ingredients are used.

Marinate for 1 week. Will keep for months in covered dish.

BOB'S GARLIC CHICKEN

ROBERT FREEMAN, JR., Napa, CA

Once you've browned the chicken, this dish will take care of itself.

14	chicken thighs
4	eggs
¾	oz. liquid garlic
1	lb. all-purpose flour
2	teaspoons salt
2	teaspoons pepper
¼	cup dehydrated garlic, or more if desired
	Olive oil
6	to 10 cloves fresh garlic, crushed
	Powdered garlic, as needed

Rinse and pat dry chicken thighs. Beat eggs and add liquid garlic. Combine flour, salt, pepper, and dehydrated garlic. Dip chicken in egg mixture then dredge in flour mixture.

In large frying pan brown thighs in 1/16 inch olive oil to which 3 to 5 crushed garlic cloves have been added. Brown until just golden on both sides. Sprinkle browning chicken with powdered garlic.

Remove browned chicken from pan and arrange in an ovenproof baking dish. Pour juices from frying pan over chicken in baking dish. Repeat procedure, being sure to add oil and crushed garlic to frying pan until all thighs have been browned and all juices added to baking dish.

Bake chicken in 350-degree oven until the meat falls off the bones. Gravy may be made from leftover juices in baking dish.

Makes 6 to 8 servings.

STUFFED CALAMARI

TIM E. JONES, San Jose, CA

Squid tubes are filled with a stuffing made with shrimp and crab, then baked in a highly seasoned tomato sauce. It won't matter if some of the filling escapes. It will all go into the sauce.

12	squid tubes, approx. 1½-inch diameter*
1	bell pepper, finely chopped
3	stalks celery, finely chopped
5	green onions, finely chopped
10	cloves fresh garlic, minced
½	lb. shrimp meat, chopped
½	lb. crabmeat, chopped**
	Juice of ½ lemon
2	tablespoons olive oil
2	cans (16 oz. *each*) tomato sauce
⅓	cup cooking sherry
2	teaspoons thyme
1	teaspoon *each* oregano, basil, garlic salt, crushed bay leaves and black pepper
1	lb. linguine, cooked and drained

Preheat oven to 350 degrees.

Rinse squid and pat dry. Mix together bell pepper, celery, onions, and garlic. Add ⅓ of mixture to shrimp and crab-meat with lemon juice. Stuff this mixture into the squid tubes and place them in a 9 × 15-inch baking dish.

Heat oil in large skillet and sauté remaining pepper, celery, onion, and garlic mixture. Add remaining ingredients and simmer 10 to 15 minutes.

Pour this sauce over the stuffed squid tubes and bake for 30 minutes.

Serve over bed of linguine. (Be sure to have some garlic bread to soak up the sauce.)

Makes 6 servings.

*Pre-cleaned squid tubes should be available at fish markets; if you can't find any just cut the tentacles off of fresh squid and clean the tubes.

**Mock crabmeat (again, available at fish markets) is just as good and considerably cheaper than the real stuff.

64

HANDMADE GARLIC-CHEESE RAVIOLI WITH GARLIC BECHAMEL SAUCE AND SHRIMP

BOB SALYERS, Monterey, CA

*T*he 1986 Cook-off finalist is a delicious blend of garlic, ricotta, and Parmesan cheese. The ravioli can be made ahead of time and frozen until you're ready for it. If you have no time to make ravioli (and have none in the freezer), try the shrimp sauce on plain linguine. The effect, of course, will not be the same, but will still be delicious.

PASTA:

3	cups flour
3	eggs, beaten
1	tablespoon olive oil
1	to 2 tablespoons water

FILLING:

24	large cloves fresh garlic, chopped
1	teaspoon Italian spices
½	teaspoon coarse black pepper
	Olive oil
1½	lb. whole milk ricotta cheese
1	cup grated fresh Parmesan cheese
¼	cup chives (fresh *or* frozen), chopped
2	eggs, beaten

SAUCE:

6	cloves fresh garlic, chopped
	Olive oil
3	tablespoons butter
3	tablespoons flour
2	cups milk
½	teaspoon salt
¼	teaspoon white pepper
1	lb. medium shrimp
1	cup grated fresh Parmesan cheese

PASTA:

Mix flour, eggs, and olive oil. Add water to proper consistency.

FILLING:

Sauté garlic, Italian spices, and black pepper in olive oil until garlic browns. Drain oil. In large bowl mix ricotta, Parmesan cheese, garlic mixture, chives, and eggs.

Roll out oblong sheets of pasta to fit ravioli form. Lay out first sheet, fill with garlic and cheese mixture. Moisten between fillings, add second sheet of pasta and roll.

May be used immediately or frozen for later use.

Boil approximately 15 minutes for fresh or 22 minutes if frozen.

SAUCE:

Sauté garlic, set aside. Melt butter over low heat (or in double boiler); stir in flour until smooth; gradually add milk. Stirring constantly, cook until sauce is thick. Stir in salt, pepper, and garlic. Use as needed, refrigerate remainder.

To Serve: With slotted spoon gently place hot ravioli on plate. Top with handful of shrimp, cover with sauce and top with fresh Parmesan cheese.

Makes 6 to 8 servings.

65

SPINACH-GARLIC PASTA WITH GARLIC-ONION SAUCE

IRA J. JACOBSON, Oakland, CA

Vidalia onions may be hard to come by (genuine Vidalias come from Vidalia, Georgia, and, according to Ira, are as sweet as apples). Spanish onions make a good substitute.

PASTA:

Place 1 cup flour in large stainless steel bowl. Make a well in the center.

Break eggs into well and add yolks and olive oil. Add spinach and garlic to which salt has been added. Mix. Work in more flour as needed. Knead until dough is smooth. Let rest.

With pasta machine, roll dough to desired thickness. Cut to desired width and cook fresh, approximately 2 minutes. Drain. Toss with sauce.

SAUCE:

Melt butter with oil in skillet; add garlic and onion. Cover and cook at medium heat until soft and clear.

Remove lid, add honey and lower heat. Cook gently about 30 minutes. Add wine and cook 5 to 10 minutes longer.

Toss with pasta and top with cheese.

Makes 2 to 4 servings.

SPINACH-GARLIC PASTA:

1½ cups all-purpose flour

2 eggs plus 4 yolks

1 tablespoon olive oil

½ lb. fresh spinach, blanched, squeezed dry and finely chopped

6 large cloves fresh garlic, crushed and finely chopped

½ teaspoon salt

GARLIC-ONION SAUCE:

½ cup butter

1 tablespoon olive oil

⅓ cup chopped fresh garlic (about 12 large cloves)

1 lb. Vidalia or other sweet onions, peeled and sliced

1 tablespoon honey

¼ cup marsala wine

Parmesan cheese

EPICUREAN EGGPLANT BAKE

ROXANNE CHAN, Albany, CA

Roxanne Chan is one of the contest's most creative cooks (she's been a finalist three years in a row). Her latest invention is a colorful concoction— meringue-topped eggplant slices surrounded by a creamy red pepper sauce.

6	large eggplant slices, ½ inch thick
2	tablespoons olive oil
½	teaspoon garlic powder

FILLING:

1	lb. Italian sausage, casings removed, crumbled
2	tablespoons butter
1	small onion, chopped
1	small head fresh garlic, cloves separated, peeled and minced
½	cup white wine
¼	cup chopped green pepper
¼	cup chopped yellow pepper
1	tomato, peeled, and seeded and diced
1	teaspoon dried oregano

MERINGUE:

1	large head fresh garlic, separated into cloves
¼	teaspoon garlic salt
4	egg whites
	Pinch of cream of tartar

CREAM:

1	large red pepper, seeded and cut into strips
½	cup cream
2	large cloves fresh garlic, peeled
⅛	teaspoon seasoned pepper
	Parsley sprigs for garnish

Brush eggplant slices with oil on both sides. Sprinkle with garlic powder.

Place slices on baking sheet and bake at 350 degrees for 30 minutes or until fork tender.

FILLING:

Combine the sausage and butter in skillet. Add onion and minced garlic. Sauté 5 minutes. Add wine, cover and simmer 10 minutes. Add peppers, tomato, and oregano. Cook uncovered 2 minutes. Cool slightly

MERINGUE:

Cook the separated garlic cloves in boiling water until soft. Peel and mash. Stir in garlic salt.

Beat egg whites with cream of tartar until stiff peaks form. Fold in garlic.

Remove eggplant from oven. Top with the filling, then cover with meringue.

Return to the oven and bake until the meringue is golden, about 15 minutes.

CREAM:

Cook red pepper strips in boiling water for 5 minutes. Drain.

Place in a blender with cream, garlic and seasoned pepper. Blend until smooth.

Place in a saucepan and heat through.

Place eggplant slices on a serving platter. Surround with pepper cream and garnish with parsley sprigs.

Makes 6 servings.

67

1987

GILROY GARLIC FESTIVAL
JULY 24·25·26 1987

There are many miracles in the world to be celebrated, and, for me, garlic is among the most deserving.

PROFESSOR LEO BUSCAGLIA

HEALTHY, HOT AND GARLICKY WINGS

WINIFRED HARANO, Los Angeles, CA

These crispy chicken wings have a special bite. They make a superb, spicy addition to your Super Bowl party buffet.

Preheat oven to 375 degrees.

Disjoint chicken wings, discarding tips, rinse and pat dry.

Separate garlic cloves and peel. Place garlic, olive oil, and Tabasco in blender or food processor and puree.

Combine Parmesan, bread crumbs, and pepper in a plastic bag.

Dip wings in the garlic puree and roll in bread crumb mixture, one at a time, coating thoroughly.

Coat a shallow nonstick baking pan with oil and add wings in a single layer. Drizzle with remaining garlic puree and sprinkle with any remaining bread crumb mixture.

Bake for 45 to 60 minutes until brown and crisp.

Makes 6 Servings.

2	lbs. chicken wings (approximately 15 wings)
3	head fresh garlic
1	cup olive oil plus 1 tablespoon
10	to 15 drops Tabasco
1	cup grated Parmesan cheese
1	cup Italian style bread crumbs
1	teaspoon black pepper

PATRICIAN ESCARGOTS

PAT TRINCHERO, Gilroy, CA

No cookbook on garlic would be complete without a recipe for escargots. This version won our judges over with its pungent, garlicky sauce and the delicious addition of baked mushroom caps.

4	heads fresh garlic
½	cup olive oil
½	cup butter
1	onion, finely chopped
1	teaspoon finely chopped fresh or dried rosemary
¼	teaspoon ground thyme
2	dashes nutmeg
	Salt and pepper to taste
24	large canned snails
½	cup chopped parsley
24	medium to large fresh mushrooms
12	pieces thin sliced white bread

Peel garlic and chop into fine pieces.

Place olive oil and butter in a frying pan over medium heat. When butter is melted, add onion, garlic, rosemary and thyme. Then add nutmeg, salt, and pepper.

Reduce heat to low and add snails and parsley; simmer for 30 minutes.

While snails are simmering, clean and remove stems from mushrooms. Arrange mushroom caps upside down in a 2 inch deep baking dish and place one snail onto each mushroom cap.

Pour garlic mixture over snails, cover with foil and bake at 350 degrees for 30 minutes.

While snails are baking, cut the crust off bread slices and cut each slice into 4 squares. Toast bread. Serve with Escargots.

Makes 4 servings.

AMBROSIAL GRAPE LEAVES

ELAINE CORRINGTON, Los Angeles, CA

A traditional recipe stands out with a generous jolt of fresh garlic. This is an appetizer that tastes right year round.

1	jar grape leaves
1	onion, chopped
2	tablespoons butter *or* olive oil
1½	lbs. ground lamb
1	to 2 heads fresh garlic, peeled and chopped
	Salt and pepper
4	to 10 oz. pine nuts (pignoli)
2	cups seedless raisins
2	to 3 tablespoons sugar
6	tablespoons cinnamon
1	stick (8 oz.) butter, melted

Rinse grape leaves, cut off stems and lay flat on work surface.

Sauté onion in butter or olive oil until translucent. Add lamb, crumbling as you cook, until done. Stir in garlic and season with salt and pepper to taste.

Remove from heat and add pine nuts, raisins, sugar, and cinnamon.

Place 2 to 3 tablespoons of the mixture in the center of each grape leaf. Fold each leaf over filling and roll up like a cigar.

Preheat oven to 350 degrees. Fill a baking dish with the stuffed grape leaves in a single layer and dribble melted butter over them. Bake for 20 minutes and serve hot.

Makes 10 servings.

GARLIC CHICKEN PINEAPPLE

B. K. KERMANI, San Jose, CA

This tangy, spicy one-pan entree is delicious served over hot steamed rice and accompanied by a good imported beer.

1	head fresh garlic, peeled
1	piece (1 inch square) fresh ginger, peeled
5	tablespoons vegetable oil
9	black peppercorns
5	cardamom pods
5	whole cloves
1	stick cinnamon
1	large onion (preferably red), chopped
1	chicken, skinned and cup up
2	potatoes, peeled and diced (optional)
1	can sliced pineapple, drained and cut in triangular pieces

70

In blender, grind garlic and ginger to form a smooth paste; add a little water for good consistency, but not too much.

Heat oil and add peppercorns, cardamom, cloves, and cinnamon, cooking until all release delectable aromas (about 3 minutes). Add onion and cook until light golden in color. Add garlic-ginger paste and cook about 5 minutes, stirring constantly. If this "masala" is sticking to the pan, add a little water and stir.

Add chicken to the masala and cook until chicken is browned. Do not worry if this masala is sticking to the pan. Reduce heat to medium.

Once chicken is browned, add about 1 cup water and deglaze pan. Reduce heat to medium low, cover pan and let chicken cook 50 minutes or until tender.

Add potatoes, if desired, after chicken has cooked 20 minutes. Just before serving, add pineapple.

Makes 4 servings.

GARLIC PUMPED CHICKEN

JOSEPH BONELLO, San Francisco, CA

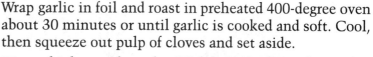

Your guests will be impressed by this elegant dish ... well worth the extra care taken in preparing it.

3	heads fresh garlic
1	chicken (3½ to 4 lbs.)
¾	lb. fresh mushrooms
8	tablespoons unsalted butter
	Salt and pepper
¼	cup chicken stock
¼	cup marsala (or port or red wine)
¼	cup heavy cream
	Juices from cavity of roasted chicken

Wrap garlic in foil and roast in preheated 400-degree oven about 30 minutes or until garlic is cooked and soft. Cool, then squeeze out pulp of cloves and set aside.

Rinse chicken and pat dry. With breast side up, beginning at the neck end, separate the skin from flesh, loosening as far into the legs and wings as possible without tearing skin. This creates a pocket for the stuffing. Set chicken aside.

Clean mushrooms and finely chop (a food processor works best). Sauté in 2 tablespoons butter over high heat until all moisture has evaporated, stirring and taking care not to burn. Cool.

Combine two-thirds of the garlic pulp, mushrooms, and remaining 6 tablespoons butter. Mix thoroughly; add salt and pepper to taste.

To stuff chicken, fill a pastry bag (use a medium tip) with garlic mixture. Insert point under skin and pump filling into pocket, spreading it evenly using your fingers. Rub outside of chicken with a little butter and sprinkle with fresh ground pepper.

Place chicken breast side up in a roasting pan with a rack and roast at 400 degrees for approximately 1½ hours until juices in thigh run clear.

Reserve juices from cavity; carefully cut up chicken into serving pieces (shears work best) and keep warm.

Prepare sauce by combining remaining third of garlic pulp and reserved juices with stock, wine, and cream in a small saucepan over high heat. Stir until thickened. Serve with chicken.

Makes 4 servings.

71

Garlic. It's the clove with clout.

LINGUINE WITH CARAMELIZED GARLIC

KIMRA FOSTER, San Jose, CA

The judges were especially taken by this creamy pasta, with its profusion of golden brown garlic cloves. The slow sautéeing process yields a sweet, rich result which has to be tasted to be believed.

3	heads fresh garlic
2	tablespoons olive oil
1	tablespoon chopped fresh thyme
⅓	cup chicken stock (if using canned, use regular, not double strength)
	Salt and pepper to taste
6	oz. linguine
2	eggs, beaten
3	oz. freshly grated Parmesan cheese

Separate garlic cloves. Immerse in boiling water for 30 seconds and peel.

Heat oil in large sauté pan over medium-low heat. Add garlic. Reduce heat to low and very slowly sauté garlic until golden brown. Stir frequently. Be careful not to burn garlic. It will take approximately 20 minutes for the garlic to reach this state.

Stir in fresh thyme. Cook 2 minutes longer. Add chicken stock, salt, and pepper. Simmer 5 minutes.

Meanwhile, cook linguine according to package directions. Drain. Toss linguine with eggs. Add to sauté pan and toss with Parmesan cheese. Adjust seasonings. Serve immediately.

Makes 3 to 4 servings.

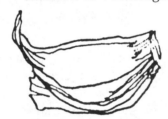

GARLIC ONION BAKE

IRA J. JACOBSON, Oakland, CA

This dish will disappear quickly at your next pot luck.

Place crackers in a bowl and pour all but two tablespoons butter over. Mix well. Press half the cracker mixture into bottom of 9 × 11 inch baking dish.

Slice onions thin and sauté with garlic in remaining butter until translucent but not brown. Place in baking dish and spread over crackers.

Grate cheese and sprinkle over garlic onion mixture.

Beat eggs and reserve. Scald milk, let cool a little and then incorporate with eggs. Pour this mixture over cheese and sprinkle remaining crackers on top.

Bake at 350 degrees for 30 minutes.

Makes 8 to 10 servings.

3	oz. soda crackers, about 35 crackers, rolled fine
3	oz. Ritz crackers, about 35 crackers, rolled fine
10	tablespoons (1¼ sticks) unsalted butter, melted
3	large red onions
1	cup chopped fresh garlic
8	oz. sharp white Cheddar cheese (no dyes)
2	eggs
1½	cups milk

NANCY'S GLORIOUS GARLIC TART

NANCY ASH, San Francisco, CA

A quiche for garlic lovers. Pack it in a basket with some fresh fruit and a bottle of chablis, and voila! ... a memorable picnic.

Pastry crust (recipe follows)

3   heads fresh garlic, cloves separated and peeled
2   teaspoons Dijon-style mustard
1   cup grated Gruyere cheese
1   egg
¼   cup heavy cream
1   teaspoon nutmeg
¼   teaspoon pepper

PASTRY CRUST:
1½   cups all purpose flour
1   teaspoon sugar
1   teaspoon salt
1   stick (8 oz.) frozen butter, cut into 6 pieces
¼   cup ice water

Half fill a large saucepan with water. Add garlic cloves and bring to a boil. Drain garlic, and repeat process with fresh water. Drain and reserve garlic.

With back of spoon, smear mustard across bottom of pastry crust, which can be hot from oven or at room temperature. Distribute cheese evenly inside crust.

In a food processor, puree reserved garlic with egg, cream, nutmeg and pepper for 30 seconds. Pour garlic mixture over cheese.

Bake tart at 350 degrees for 25 minutes, until filling is firm. Serve hot or at room temperature.

CRUST:

Preheat oven to 350 degrees.

In food processor, combine flour, sugar, salt, and butter until mixture looks crumbly. With motor running, slowly add water. Mixture will gather into a ball.

Wrap dough in plastic wrap and refrigerate for at least ½ hour.

Butter and flour inside of a 9-inch tart pan with removable bottom. Roll out dough to fit into pan. Trim edges. Line dough with foil and fill center with pie weights or dried beans.

Bake for 20 minutes. Remove foil and weights. Continue baking crust for additional 10 minutes, until crust begins to brown.

Makes 8 servings.

73

1988

10th Annual

Gilroy Garlic Festival

JULY
29·30·31
1988

*Gilroy gives gargantuan
gastronomic gathering for garlic.*

SAN JOSE MERCURY NEWS

JOHN BAUTISTA-STYLE GARLICKY STUFFED CHICKEN WINGS

JOHN BAUTISTA, Morgan Hill, CA

We think these are the best fried chicken wings you'll ever taste. Serve with a ready-made Asian dipping sauce from the supermarket, or make your own.

Remove large bone in chicken wing being careful not to cut the outer skin.

Stuff cavity with meat and garlic (garlic to taste).

Dip stuffed wings in tempura batter. Fry in very hot oil. Cook until golden brown. Remove from oil and drain on paper towels. Serve hot.

Very good when served with dipping sauce.

Makes 4 servings.

12	chicken wings (approximately 2 lbs.)
½	lb. Chinese-type barbecued pork (*or* cooked ham)
1	medium-sized garlic bulb
1	quart cooking oil
	Tempura batter

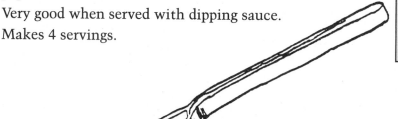

EGGPLANT ANTIPASTA

RUDY and GLORIA MELONE, San Francisco, CA

Serve this fresh-tasting appetizer in the summer ... with vine-ripened tomatoes and basil from your own backyard. It's so easy and delicious, you'll find yourself making it again and again.

4	to 6 eggplants (Chinese or Japanese)
4	tomatoes, chopped
1	bulb garlic, crushed or finely chopped
	Fresh basil, finely chopped *or* dried
	Olive oil
	Salt and pepper to taste
	Parmesan cheese, grated (optional)

Cut eggplant in half, lengthwise, then again crosswise so you end up with 4 pieces. Make a couple of slits on the meat of the eggplant without cutting through to the skin.

Stuff chopped tomatoes into the slits of the eggplant, place garlic on top and sprinkle with basil. Sprinkle with Parmesan cheese, if so desired. Drizzle with lots of olive oil.

Bake in a pan at 350 degrees for 25 to 30 minutes.

Serves 4–6 as an appetizer.

BETTY JAYNE'S GARLIC SOUP

MRS. BETTY JAYNE JONES, Longview, WA

This hearty soup makes a warming first course on a cold winter's night.

4	tablespoons olive oil
30	large cloves fresh garlic, peeled and chopped
2	cans chicken broth, about 1 quart
2	cups water
2	cans (15 oz. *each*) canellini beans
1	teaspoon *each* salt and pepper
2	bay leaves
1	fresh jalapeño pepper, seeded and chopped
1	cup whipping cream
12	slices French bread
	Parmesan cheese, grated

In saucepan, heat oil over medium heat. Add garlic and sauté until soft and golden. Add chicken broth, water, beans, salt, pepper, bay leaves, and jalapeño pepper. Simmer 5 minutes.

Pour into blender and puree. Return to saucepan. Stir in cream and heat through.

Toast bread lightly. Sprinkle with Parmesan cheese and broil 3 minutes or until cheese is golden and bubbly. Serve toast in soup.

Makes 8 cups.

FORTY CLOVE CHICKEN FILICE

VAL FILICE, Gilroy, CA

Garlic, lemon, and chicken combine for a flavor we never tire of. This dish was selected a winner for its straightforward goodness and the "something extra" contributed by the vermouth and spices.

Place chicken pieces into shallow baking pan, skin side up. Sprinkle all ingredients evenly over top of chicken. Squeeze juice from lemon and pour over top. Cut remaining lemon rind into pieces and arrange throughout chicken.

Cover with foil and bake at 375 degrees for 40 minutes. Remove foil and bake an additional 15 minutes.

Serves 4.

1	frying chicken, cut in pieces
40	cloves fresh garlic
½	cup dry white wine
¼	cup dry vermouth
¼	cup olive oil
4	stalks celery, cut in 1-inch pieces
1	teaspoon oregano
2	teaspoons dry basil
6	sprigs minced parsley
	Pinch of crushed red pepper
1	lemon
	Salt and pepper to taste

76

HOMEMADE ITALIAN SAUSAGE

BOB McHAM, DON GAGE and DICK BOZZO, Gilroy, CA

Homemade sausages aren't as laborious to assemble as most people may think, and the mouth-watering results are well worth the effort.

Grind pork roast with a coarse grind sausage blade. Add salt, black pepper, garlic, chile peppers, and the options desired.

Knead this mixture thoroughly for at least 10 minutes. When mixed properly, the mixture will stick to your hand for 3 or 4 seconds when held upside down.

Wash the casings in water thoroughly, inside and out. Tie one end closed and then pack the ingredients inside the casing tightly, making sure to remove all air and filling voids. Tie the other end closed. About every 4 or 5 inches, pinch the filled casing together and double the end back through in a looping motion. This will divide your sausage into individual connected pieces.

With a fork, prick each segment 3 or 4 times. Place the sausage in an uncovered container and refrigerate them for 3 days. This allows the ingredients to "marry."

Sausage can now be stored, dried or frozen.

Makes approximately 16 sausages.

9	lbs. Boston butt pork roast, boned
3	oz. salt
3	tablespoons black pepper
¼	cup fresh garlic, finely chopped
3	tablespoons crushed red chile pepper
	Casings—pork small intestines
2	tablespoons fennel (optional)
1	tablespoon oregano (optional)

Now the pungent bulb is back in favor, its nervy aroma drifting from the best kitchens to enhance many a little dinner party.

TOWN AND COUNTRY

77

SCAMPI ALLA "FIREMAN CHEF"

JIM NEIL, Alameda, CA

Bay Area fireman Jim Neil brings a fresh, five-alarm taste to a traditional favorite.

Shell and devein the prawns. Rinse and set aside.

Reserve a few nice sprigs of parsley for garnish and mince the rest.

Heat the clarified butter in a large sauté pan over medium heat. Lightly sauté the garlic for 1 to 2 minutes, being careful not to let it brown.

Add the prawns, scallions, lemon juice, and wine. Cook the mixture until the prawns turn pink and firm, a minute or two on each side. *Be careful not to overcook.* At the last minute, add the minced parsley and season with salt and pepper.

Serve the scampi on individual shells or small gratin dishes, garnished with a slice or two of lemon and a fresh parsley sprig.

Serves 4–6 as an appetizer.

1	lb. large prawns
8	sprigs fresh parsley
⅓	cup clarified butter
4	tablespoons minced garlic
6	scallions, thinly sliced
	Juice of one lemon (approximately 2 tablespoons)
¼	cup dry white wine
	Salt and freshly ground pepper, to taste
	Lemon slices for garnish

TECHNICOLOR GARLIQUE SHRIMP

LORI SHULA, Reseda, CA

Make this dish in the summer, when bell peppers are sweetest and their colors bright. The garlic and chile paste ensure that the flavor is as vibrant as the colors.

78

1	full head garlic (about 12 large cloves)
16	large raw shrimp
3	large bell peppers, 1 *each* red, yellow, and green
3	tablespoons vegetable oil
¼	lb. butter
¼	cup Chinese chile paste
2	cups cooked rice

Blanch garlic cloves in boiling water 3 minutes. Drain, peel and slice. Set aside.

Peel and devein shrimp and slice in half lengthwise. Set aside.

Seed and cut peppers into ½ inch strips.

Heat oil and butter in large heavy skillet. Over high heat, sauté peppers, tossing and stirring for 1 minute. Add shrimp and continue to toss and stir just until shrimp turn pink. Stir in sliced garlic and chile paste. Taste sauce and adjust seasoning.

Serve over hot rice. Makes 4 servings.

FESTIVE SPINACH FETTUCCINE IN CREAMY GARLIC CHEESE SAUCE (very tangy)

DEBBIE CLYMENS, Oakley, CA

The secret that makes this recipe a winner is allowing the cream cheese to melt very slowly—never letting it bubble. The colors make it a perfect complement for your holiday goose.

1	to 2 tablespoons olive oil
¼	cup chopped chives *or* green onion tops
1	or more heads fresh garlic, peeled and chopped
⅛	cup vinegar *or* dry white wine
1	to 2 packages (8 oz. *each*) cream cheese
½	lb. fresh *or* dry spinach fettuccine
1	large fresh red bell pepper, diced
1	can (16 oz.) large whole pitted ripe olives, drained
	Parsley *or* Carrot curls for garnish

In sauté pan, add olive oil and chopped chives and half the chopped garlic. Then add vinegar or wine. Sauté for about 5 minutes, then add cream cheese; lower heat and allow cheese to melt very slowly.

Cook fettuccine in boiling water until just done *al dente*. Drain. Add bell pepper, remaining garlic, and olives and toss lightly.

Lay out on serving platter and pour sauce over. Garnish with parsley or carrot curls.

Makes 4 servings.

79

1989

Gilroy Garlic Festival

July 28, 29, 30, 1989

The main attraction was the cooking contest and it was a doozy.
The winners were real winners.

FOOD AND WINE MAGAZINE

GARLIC PESTO CHEESE PUFFS

PATRICE TORRESANI, Fremont, CA

*Cook these savory tidbits just before your guests are due to arrive.
The sensation of biting through the crispy outside into the warm, garlicky filling
is irresistible ... they won't last long!*

4	cups vegetable oil
1	cup flour
1	tablespoon sugar
1	teaspoon baking powder
1	teaspoon dried parsley
1	lb. ricotta cheese
2	eggs
10	cloves fresh garlic, finely chopped
2	teaspoons pesto (e.g. Christopher Ranch brand)
½	cup grated fresh Parmesan cheese

Heat oil in frying pan to 375 degrees.

Meanwhile, mix flour, sugar, baking powder and parsley in large bowl. Add ricotta cheese, eggs, garlic, and pesto. Mix thoroughly.

Drop by tablespoonsful into hot oil and cook until puffed. Brown on all sides, turning as needed. Remove and drain well on paper towels.

Place on warm platter and sprinkle with Parmesan cheese.

Makes approximately 2 dozen puffs.

81

AROMATIC ROSE CHICKEN AND FENNEL SALAD

BARBARA J. MORGAN, Concord, CA

This fresh-tasting cold chicken salad, with the beguiling flavors of fennel and citrus, is wonderful served for lunch on the patio with a tall glass of iced tea.

2   tablespoons butter
1   cup raw rice
4   cups chicken broth
4   chicken half breasts, boned and skinned
3   whole heads fresh garlic
2   cloves garlic, minced
½   cup diced fennel bulb
1   red pepper, diced
6   marinated artichoke hearts, cut up
1   can (4.25 oz.) chopped black olives
1   crisp apple, peeled and diced

VINAIGRETTE:
4   tablespoons orange juice
4   teaspoons lemon juice
1   teaspoon vinegar
½   teaspoon salt
2   cloves garlic, crushed
3   minced scallions (white part only)
¼   teaspoon fennel seeds, crushed
5   tablespoons olive oil
1   tablespoon *each* chopped chives, fennel leaves, and parsley

Melt 1 tablespoon butter in sauté pan. Add rice and cook, stirring until rice turns golden. Add 2 cups chicken broth to pan, cover and reduce heat. Simmer until rice absorbs liquid. Pour rice in bowl to cool.

Place chicken breasts and 3 heads garlic in saucepan. Add remaining 2 cups chicken broth and cook for 20 to 25 minutes until chicken is tender. Remove chicken and allow to cool.

Remove garlic, peel and place in frying pan with 1 tablespoon butter, 2 cloves minced garlic, diced fennel bulb and red pepper. Stir-fry 2 to 3 minutes. Add to cooked rice.

Dice chicken meat and add to rice along with artichoke hearts, olives, and diced apple. Mix well and pour citrus vinaigrette over all. Refrigerate until well chilled.

Garnish salad with strips of red bell pepper, cut julienned, if desired.

Makes 6 servings.

CITRUS VINAIGRETTE:

Combine orange juice, lemon juice, and vinegar in food processor with salt, garlic cloves, scallions, and fennel seeds.

Blend in olive oil. Pour in bowl. Add chives, chopped fennel leaves, and finely chopped parsley and blend well.

82

SKEWERED CHICKEN AND GARLIC

PRISCILLA YEE, Concord, CA

Grilled marinated garlic cloves on skewers with chicken and fresh vegetables were a combination the judges couldn't resist. You won't believe how good this simple-to-make recipe tastes.

MARINADE:

¼ cup white wine

¼ cup lime juice

¼ cup chopped fresh basil leaves *or* 4 teaspoons dried basil

2 jalapeño peppers, seeded, minced

2 tablespoons olive oil

6 cloves fresh garlic, peeled, chopped

1 tablespoon peeled, minced ginger root

1 tablespoon soy sauce

2 teaspoon sugar

SKEWERS:

24 whole cloves fresh garlic

6 chicken breast halves, skinned, boned

2 red bell peppers, cut into 1-inch chunks

2 cups seeded, diced Roma tomatoes

¼ cup sliced green onions

2 tablespoons chopped cilantro

Salt

Basil leaves, cilantro sprigs, and lime slices for garnish

Combine marinade ingredients in small bowl; pour into large plastic bag.

Drop whole garlic cloves into boiling water; boil 10 minutes (parboiling the garlic cloves leaves them mild enough to eat, but still firm enough to skewer). Drain, cool slightly. Peel and add to marinade.

Cut chicken into 1½ inch cubes; add to marinade. Seal bag and refrigerate at least 1 hour or overnight.

Thread chicken, garlic cloves, and bell pepper chunks alternately onto skewers. Grill or broil 4 inches from heat for 6 minutes or until chicken is browned and cooked through.

Meanwhile, pour marinade into saucepan; bring to a boil over medium heat. Stir in tomatoes, green onions, cilantro, and salt to taste; remove from heat.

Serve with chicken. Garnish with basil or cilantro sprigs and lime slices, if desired.

Makes 6 servings.

83

GRILLED TURKEY TENDERLOINS IN GARLIC-ANCHO CHILE SAUCE

ALAN C. DELL'ARIO, Oakland, CA

This delicious mole-style sauce has traditionally been served with chicken in southwestern cuisine. The turkey tenderloins make an elegant, healthful alternative.

Stem and seed chiles. Heat water and pour over chiles. Let stand for at least 30 minutes.

Heat oil in large saucepan. Sauté onion and garlic until tender, *not brown*, about 5 minutes.

Add tomatillos, chiles, and ½ cup of chile liquid. Add Worcestershire sauce, sugar, chocolate chips, cinnamon, and cumin. Simmer for 20 minutes. Add salt and pepper to taste.

Pour into food processor or food mill and puree; then strain through a medium sieve. Sauce should be thick. This sauce can be made 2 days ahead.

At least 2 hours before serving, trim turkey tenderloins and pour sauce over them in a tight-fitting, covered container to marinate.

Remove turkey from sauce. Reserve all sauce and set aside ½ cup for basting. Grill turkey tenderloins until just done, about 4 to 5 minutes per side, over hot charcoal or under broiler, basting with ½ cup sauce.

Heat remaining reserved sauce and pass with cooked turkey. Garnish with chopped cilantro.

Makes 4 servings.

4	dried Ancho or Pasilla chiles
1	cup water
1	tablespoon olive oil
1	onion, chopped
8	cloves fresh garlic, minced
2	tomatillos, chopped
2	tablespoons Worcestershire sauce
1	tablespoon sugar
1	tablespoon chocolate chips
1	1 teaspoon cinnamon
1	teaspoon cumin
	Salt and pepper to taste
4	to 8 turkey tenderloins, about 1½ to 2 lb.
1	cup fresh cilantro, chopped

F.B.I. FRIED CHICKEN
(Full Blooded Italian Fried Chicken)

PATRICIA TRINCHERO, Gilroy, CA

J. Edgar Hoover himself would have given the prize for this awarding dish.

4	lbs. chicken thighs
2	cups flour
2	tablespoons granulated garlic
1	teaspoon coarsely chopped dried oregano
½	teaspoon salt
½	teaspoon pepper
1	cup olive oil
4	heads fresh garlic
¾	cup butter
2	tablespoons finely chopped fresh rosemary
½	cup finely chopped mushrooms
	Sourdough bread

Rinse and pat chicken dry. Combine flour, granulated garlic, oregano, salt and pepper. Coat chicken with flour mixture.

Heat 1 cup olive oil to moderately high heat and fry chicken until skin is crisp (chicken should not be thoroughly cooked).

Meanwhile, chop fresh garlic. Heat the butter in a large covered skillet; add chopped garlic, rosemary and mushrooms and simmer for 5 to 10 minutes. Add chicken to the garlic butter and cover. Continue to cook over low heat for 45 minutes. Stir occasionally.

Garnish and serve with crispy bread.

Makes 8 servings.

COLLEEN'S
GARLICKY BAKED SALMON

COLLEEN WEISS, Purling, NY

The easiest way we know to cook salmon. Just sprinkle with the seasonings, stick in the oven, and the flavors take care of themselves.

1	to 1½ lbs. salmon fillets
½	stick butter, cut into ¼-inch pats, plus 3 tablespoons
	Salt and pepper to taste
1	medium onion
1	lemon
1	large head fresh garlic, peeled and separated into cloves
1	package of Good Season's Italian Salad Dressing Mix
2	tablespoons oil
2	tablespoons water
	Parsley

Butter sides and bottom of baking pan with 3 tablespoons butter.

Lay fish fillets in pan, top each with a pat of butter. Salt and pepper to taste. Cut onion in thin rings and place over fish. Sprinkle garlic cloves around fish.

Take ½ lemon, squeeze over fish. Cut remaining half into slices and place over fish. Mix salad dressing mix with oil and water. Pour over fish.

Bake at 350 degrees for 30 to 40 minutes. Sprinkle with chopped fresh parsley and serve.

Makes 4 servings.

85

SLAM'S PRAWNS DULCE PARA JULIE

SLAM CAMPBELL, Chico, CA

Constant turning while grilling and basting with the sweet, spicy marinade are winning techniques for this finalist in the cook-off. Be sure to serve the prawns hot off the grill with the cool foil of freshly sliced avocado.

½	lb. fresh large prawns
⅔	cup honey
⅔	cup Rhine wine (*or other sweet, fruity wine*)
10	large cloves fresh garlic
½	teaspoon Worcestershire sauce
½	teaspoon vinegar
½	teaspoon hot mustard powder (Chinese style)
2	cups water
1	teaspoon salt
¼	cup butter
1	cup long grain white rice
¾	cup chopped green onions
⅓	cup chopped red bell pepper
¼	teaspoon ground black pepper
½	avocado, sliced in strips ¼-inch thick

Clean and peel prawns, cover and place in refrigerator.

Prepare marinade by mixing together honey and ⅓ cup wine in medium-sized mixing bowl. Crush 4 garlic cloves into honey/wine mixture, then stir in Worcestershire sauce, vinegar, and mustard powder. Cover prawns with marinade and refrigerate.

Meanwhile, preheat barbecue (Weber kettle works best). Prawns will be cooked over low heat so use small amount of briquettes.

While coals are heating, prepare rice. In saucepan, bring water, salt, and butter to a boil. Add rice, remaining 6 cloves garlic (crushed), onions, bell pepper, wine and black pepper. Cover saucepan, reduce heat and let simmer for 20 minutes.

When coals are ready, place prawns on 4 metal skewers. Cook over open barbecue, basting and turning constantly. Cook until prawns are reddish in color, about 7 minutes.

To serve, place rice in long row in each of 4 plates. Top with avocado slices. Carefully remove prawns from skewers and place on top of rice. Serve with garlic bread and salad (crab salad with honey mustard dressing is ideal).

Makes 4 servings.

ONION AND ROASTED GARLIC PIE

MARK R. BOYER, Altamone Springs, FL

Sweet onions and roasted garlic combine for a surprisingly mild, rich quiche! Bake individual tartlets for an elegant appetizer.

Sauté onions in butter until golden brown. Add roasted garlic. Let cool to room temperature.

In large mixing bowl, whisk together eggs and sour cream. Add onions and garlic. Season with salt and pepper and mix well. Pour into unbaked pie shell and top with Parmesan cheese.

Bake for 20 minutes in preheated 450 degree oven. Turn heat down to 325 degrees and finish baking for 20 minutes. Remove from oven and allow to set a few minutes before cutting.

Makes 6 servings.

*Vidialia or Walla Walla sweet onions are best.

ROASTED GARLIC:

Peel outer skin layers of 3 whole heads fresh garlic leaving heads intact. Place all heads on double thickness of foil; top with 1½ tablespoons butter and 2 sprigs fresh rosemary *or* oregano (or 1 teaspoon dried). Fold up and seal.

Bake in 375 degrees oven 55 to 60 minutes.

Squeeze cloves from skins and set aside. Discard skins.

4	yellow onions,* julienned
4	oz. sweet cream butter
3	heads roasted fresh garlic (see below)
3	eggs
8	oz. sour cream
1	teaspoon kosher salt
10	turns cracked black pepper
1	pie shell, unbaked
3	oz. Parmesan cheese

87

BOB & LEE'S THREE GARLIC PASTA

ROB KROL and LEE OHANIAN, Northridge, CA

This garlicky trio brings new vigor to ordinary smoked chicken—fresh herbs and wine in a light and creamy sauce make for an Italian winner!

1	whole chicken breast
2	large heads fresh garlic
1½	tablespoons olive oil
1½	tablespoons butter
¼	cup red onion, chopped
1	large fresh tomato, peeled, seeded and chopped
¼	teaspoon thyme
⅛	teaspoon white pepper
	Salt and pepper, freshly ground, to taste
¼	cup dry white wine
¼	cup chicken stock
½	cup heavy cream
8	to 12 oz. cooked pasta (spaghetti, linguine, etc.)
	Parsley, freshly chopped

In a smoker, using hickory chips, smoke the chicken breast and 1 head of garlic for 2 to 3 hours, depending on the amount of chicken. Or substitute already smoked chicken and roast 1 head garlic (see recipe below).

In a cast iron skillet, sauté 8 finely chopped garlic cloves and onion in olive oil and butter until golden. Shred smoked chicken; combine with sautéed garlic and onion in skillet.

Add smoked garlic by "squeezing" the cloves. Discard skins. Add tomato, thyme, white pepper, salt and pepper to taste. Add dry white wine and chicken stock. Cook over medium heat for 5 minutes, uncovered.

Add heavy cream and cook over low heat for 8 minutes, uncovered. Add 3 (or to taste) finely chopped raw fresh garlic cloves. Serve over pasta.

Garnish with finely chopped parsley.

Makes 2 servings.

ROASTED GARLIC:

Peel outer skin layers from head of fresh garlic, leaving cloves and head intact. Place head on double thickness of foil; brush with 1 teaspoon olive oil. Fold up and seal.

Bake in 375 degrees oven 45 to 55 minutes. Squeeze cloves from skins and set aside. Discard skins.

SUNNY GARLIC CHUTNEY

JEFF DENBO, Encino, CA

This aromatic accompaniment is well worth the effort!
Spice up cold meats and breads with this pungent tapenade.

200 +	fresh garlic cloves, about one quart
1	onion, diced
1	red pepper, diced
1¼	cups apple cider vinegar
¼	cup fresh ginger, minced
1	tablespoon mustard seed
1	teaspoon salt
¼	teaspoon crushed red pepper

Coarsely chop garlic. Combine all other ingredients and bring to a slow boil. Reduce by one third, add garlic and cook about ten minutes. Cool and serve.

Makes about 2½ cups.

Eat leeks in tide and garlic in May, and all the year after physicians may play.
RUSSIAN PROVERB

89

1990

GILROY GARLIC
FESTIVAL
July 27, 28, 29, 1990

GARLIC FESTIVAL
OUTDOES SUPERBOWL

AMSTERDAM NEW YORK *RECORDER*

GARLIC AND CORN SOUP

AMY KACZMARZYK, Santa Cruz, CA

Be sure to use fresh sweet corn for this aromatic soup, redolent of the flavors of Mexico. A squeeze of fresh lime adds an authentic touch.

16	cloves fresh garlic, minced
1	medium onion
2	tablespoons butter
¼	teaspoon red pepper flakes
2	tablespoons cumin
1	tablespoon coriander
3	cups fresh corn kernels
2	stalks celery, diced
1	carrot, diced
4	cups chicken stock
2	red bell peppers, roasted, peeled and diced
2	Anaheim chiles, roasted, peeled and diced
2	tablespoons olive oil
1	tablespoon chopped cilantro
1	cup black olives, chopped
1	teaspoon salt or to taste
	Juice of 1 lime

In a pot large enough for the finished soup, sauté half the garlic with onion in butter until onions are translucent. Add red pepper flakes, cumin, coriander, 2 cups corn, celery, and carrot. Sauté 5 minutes.

Add chicken stock and half the bell peppers and chiles. Bring to a boil, reduce heat and cover. Simmer 15 to 20 minutes or until the vegetables are soft.

While soup simmers, caramelize (brown) the reserved minced garlic in olive oil in a small skillet. Remove garlic and set aside.

Sauté reserved corn in remaining oil until soft.

Puree vegetable and stock mixture in a blender, in batches, until smooth and return to pot. Add caramelized garlic, reserved bell peppers, chiles and corn, olives and cilantro. Season to taste with salt and lime juice. Heat through and serve.

Makes 4 to 6 servings.

91

PRESTO PESTO SOUP

SONIA GOLDSMITH, San Francisco, CA

What an inspiration! The flavors of pesto translated into savory, light soup. This is the perfect first course for any Italian meal.

6	cups water
	Vegetable bouillon, (preferably chicken-flavored vegetarian) to make 6 cups
1½	cups basil leaves
½	small onion
	Juice of ½ lemon
¼	cup pine nuts
¼	cup grated Parmesan cheese
15	cloves fresh garlic, peeled
2	tablespoons olive oil
	Cracked pepper to taste
6	Roma tomatoes, peeled, seeded and diced
8	very thin slices fresh mozzarella cheese

In soup pot, bring water to a boil. Add bouillon and mix well. Add basil, onion, lemon juice, pine nuts, Parmesan, 12 cloves garlic, olive oil, and pepper. Cook together, about 10 minutes.

Cool, pour into blender and blend thoroughly.

Return to soup pot. Add tomatoes and reserved 3 cloves garlic, which have been sliced. Cook for 5 more minutes and serve.

Garnish with mozzarella cheese, if desired.

Makes 8 servings.

SPICY SUCCULENT TURKEY LEGS

GENEVIEVE MARCUS, Beverly Hills, CA

Slow, long cooking brings out the flavor of the garlic and herbs, and makes the meat tender and succulent. This is comfort food—perfect for supper on a rainy winter's day.

Skin turkey drumsticks and place in a nonplastic container with tight-fitting lid. Pour wine over turkey and sprinkle with half the pepper, salt, rosemary, tarragon, sage, and onion powder. Add garlic cloves and cover dish. Let marinate for 2 hours (uncooked meat should be marinated in refrigerator for safety's sake).

Turn drumsticks over and sprinkle with remaining herbs and spices. Redistribute garlic evenly and marinate for 2 more hours or overnight.

Transfer turkey and marinade (including garlic) to covered baking dish; bake at 350 degrees for 2 hours.

Note: Turkey can also be cooked on top of stove, covered, over medium/low heat.

Turn meat halfway through cooking time. There should be plenty of gravy and meat should fall off the bones easily. Vegetables or cut-up potatoes may be added during the last half hour of cooking time, if desired.

Makes 2 servings.

2	turkey drumsticks (12 oz. each)
1	to 2 cups dry red or white wine
1	teaspoon black pepper
1	teaspoon salt
2	teaspoon dried rosemary leaves
1	teaspoon dried tarragon leaves
1	teaspoon dried sage leaves
1	teaspoon onion powder
8	to 12 cloves fresh garlic

INDONESIAN CHICKEN WITH GREEN BEANS AND GARLIC

ELMER SCHOON, Excelsior, MN

Garlic is a key ingredient for any stir-fry, in our opinion. This one made an impression on the judges in 1990, with its inspired combination of spices.

1	lb. green beans, trimmed and cut into bite-sized pieces
3	tablespoons olive oil
6	chicken breast halves, boned and skinned, about 6 oz. each, cut into bite-sized pieces
10	cloves fresh garlic, minced
1	tablespoon minced fresh ginger root
1	small onion, chopped
	Juice of 1 lime *or* 1 small lemon (lime preferred)
1	tablespoon double black soy sauce*
1	teaspoon brown sugar
2	teaspoons turmeric
1	teaspoon salt
½	cup water
	Hot cooked rice

Steam green beans until just tender; do not overcook. Set aside.

Heat 2 tablespoons oil in wok or sauté pan and sauté chicken until meat turns white and is cooked through; set aside.

Heat remaining 1 tablespoon oil and sauté garlic, ginger, and onion until onion is soft. Do not let garlic burn. Stir in green beans. Add lime juice, soy sauce, brown sugar, turmeric, salt, and ¼ cup water; let simmer for a few seconds. Remaining water can be added if necessary, but sauce should not be thin.

Add chicken pieces and stir until heated through and well coated with sauce. Serve over rice.

Makes 6 servings.

*DOUBLE BLACK SOY SAUCE:

Available at Oriental food stores or you can make your own by mixing 2 teaspoons of regular soy sauce with 1 teaspoon dark molasses.

93

BUTTERFLIED LEG OF LAMB WITH ROASTED GARLIC AND TOMATO SAUCE

DONNA BERSAGLIERI, Oakland, CA

Lamb lovers and garlic lovers alike will applaud this sumptuous entree, beautifully complemented by the smooth, rich sauce.

5	to 6 lb. leg of lamb, boned and butterflied
½	lemon
2	cloves fresh garlic, cut in slivers
	Rosemary leaves, preferably fresh
1	teaspoon salt
4	tablespoons olive oil *or* other vegetable oil
5	to 6 whole heads fresh garlic
¾	cup peeled and diced fresh plum *or* other tomatoes
1½	tablespoons Balsamic vinegar *or* red wine vinegar
1	teaspoon paprika
	Salt and pepper
½	to ¾ cup heavy cream
	Chopped parsley
	Fresh rosemary sprigs (optional)

Rub lamb with cut lemon and make incisions in the meat in several places. Insert garlic slivers and a few rosemary leaves in each cut. Combine salt and pepper and rub all over meat; do the same with the oil. Let marinate for 2 to 3 hours.

Meanwhile, place heads of garlic in greased shallow baking pan and bake at 325 degrees for 35 to 45 minutes or until cloves are soft. Remove from pan and allow to cool slightly.

Squeeze garlic pulp from each clove and place in food processor or blender. Add tomatoes, vinegar and paprika and blend until smooth. Transfer to a saucepan.

Cook mixture over moderate heat for 10 minutes, then slowly whisk in cream. Continue to simmer for 5 to 10 minutes. Season to taste with salt and pepper. Sauce may be made ahead and reheated.

Roast lamb at 325 degrees until internal temperature reaches 135 degrees for rare or 160 degrees for medium meat. Remove lamb from oven and cover loosely with foil. Allow to rest for 10 to 15 minutes before slicing.

Pour warm sauce onto heated platter and arrange lamb slices over sauce. Sprinkle with chopped parsley and garnish with sprigs of fresh rosemary, if desired.

Makes 6 to 8 servings.

94

ROAST PORK STRIPS WITH GARLIC

BETTY ENG, Colorado Springs, CO

The honey glaze on these pork strips gives them a crispy sweetness that is deliciously complemented by the Asian flavors in the sauce. Nutlike cloves of roasted garlic add the finishing touch.

10	lbs. pork butt
¼	cup rice wine *or* dry sherry
2½	teaspoons salt
3⅓	tablespoons sugar
5	tablespoons dark soy sauce
3	tablespoons regular soy sauce
3	cloves fresh garlic, minced
1	tablespoon minced fresh ginger root
1	teaspoon sesame oil
½	teaspoon ground white pepper
¼	teaspoon ground ginger
¼	cup honey mixed with 2 tablespoons water, for glaze
1	tablespoon fresh coriander leaves, finely chopped
4	whole heads fresh garlic
	Walnut oil

Cut pork into long strips lengthwise, 2 inches wide. Rub meat with rice wine; then salt. Combine sugar, dark and regular soy sauce, garlic, ginger root, ground ginger, sesame oil, and white pepper and rub into meat.

Place meat in a nonplastic container, cover and marinate in refrigerator for at least 1 hour, but not more than 4 hours.

Preheat oven to 350 degrees and set meat on a rack over a roasting pan. Roast for 30 minutes.

Place whole heads of garlic in pan under meat and turn meat over. Roast for another 15 minutes or until edges of meat appear crisp and brown.

Using a brush, apply a thin coating of the honey glaze onto meat strips and roast an additional 10 minutes. Turn off heat and remove pork. Allow meat to cool slightly before cutting into ¼-inch thick slices.

Pour meat drippings into a small saucepan, reserving garlic heads. Add enough water to make one cup. Warm over low heat and add chopped coriander.

Break whole heads of garlic into cloves, sprinkle with walnut oil and serve with pork. Diners squeeze the pulp onto meat. Pass sauce with pork.

Makes 6 servings.

The best thing to do with garlic of course, is to eat it.

SYLVIA RUBIN
SAN FRANCISCO CHRONICLE

95

ORIGINAL CAJUN GOURMET BURGER

RONALD C. TREADWAY, SR., Acworth, GA

Guaranteed to be a hit at your next barbecue! Have the kids help you make these burgers, and be sure to prepare them a day ahead to let the flavors come out.

2	lbs. ground chuck *or* sirloin
1	large yellow onion, chopped
6	or more cloves fresh garlic, minced
1	medium bell pepper, chopped
1	bunch green onions, white bulb and half of green tops, chopped
1	large egg
2	tablespoons Worcestershire sauce
1	tablespoon soy sauce
¼	teaspoon Tabasco sauce
¼	teaspoon coarsely ground black pepper
¼	teaspoon salt
¼	teaspoon dry mustard
¼	teaspoon seasoned salt
¼	teaspoon dried thyme
¼	teaspoon cornstarch
1	tablespoon softened cream cheese
1	tablespoon plain dry bread crumbs

In a large bowl, combine all ingredients. Combine well, by hand, and shape into patties. If desired, place burger in an airtight container and refrigerate overnight to let flavors intensify.

Bake, broil, fry, or grill burgers the way you like them, medium or well done, and serve as a main course or in a bun with your favorite garnishes.

Makes 6 to 8 servings.

Imagine a world without garlic. No spaghetti sauce. No veal parmigiana. No ratatouille. No Chinese cooking, Italian cooking, or Greek cooking. No Fun.

SAVANNAH NEWS

SHRIMP IN FRESH TOMATO MANGO SALSA

MARK DOUGLAS, Riverside, CA

*T*he judges were dazzled by the beautiful presentation as well as the fresh flavors of this Caribbean-inspired dish. Wait until fresh mangoes are in the market and serve as a main dish or cut the recipe in half to serve 6 as an appetizer.

4	large, ripe tomatoes (preferably beefsteak), peeled and diced
4	Anaheim chiles, roasted, peeled, seeded and chopped
2	large mangoes, peeled and cut into bite-sized chunks
1	head fresh garlic, about 15 cloves, peeled and chopped fine
½	cup white wine vinegar
¾	cup chopped fresh cilantro
	Coarse (kosher) salt and hot pepper sauce (preferably Tabasco) to taste
3	tablespoons avocado oil
2	medium onions, peeled and chopped
2	lbs. shrimp, trimmed, peeled and deveined
⅓	cup brandy
5	cups cooked rice
	Cilantro sprigs for garnish

In a large bowl, combine tomatoes, Anaheim chiles, half the mango chunks, half the chopped garlic, vinegar, and cilantro. Add salt and dashes of red hot pepper sauce to taste. Cover and chill.

In a large skillet, heat avocado oil until hot, but not smoking. Sauté onions for about one minute and add remaining garlic and shrimp. Cook about one minute, pour brandy over and stir well, cooking just until shrimp turn pink. Remove from heat and set aside.

Gently fold shrimp mixture into cool salsa and turn out onto large platter or divide between 6 dinner plates. Place remaining mango chunks on top of shrimp. Arrange hot cooked rice around circumference of platter or place rice next to shrimp on individual plates. Garnish with sprigs of cilantro, if desired.

Makes 6 servings.

97

PASTA WITH GROUND VENISON AND ROASTED GARLIC

LORI FILICE, Gilroy, CA

If you don't have venison ground lamb works beautifully in this hearty pasta. Serve with crusty Italian bread to sop up the sauce.

2	tablespoons olive oil
½	cup chopped onion
1	lb. ground venison *or* lamb
2	cups dry red wine
1	tablespoon chopped fresh rosemary *or* 2 teaspoons dried
1	tablespoon chopped fresh oregano *or* 2 teaspoons dried
1	tablespoon chopped fresh basil *or* 2 teaspoons dried
4	tomatoes, seeded, pureed, excess juice reserved
5	heads roasted garlic (recipe follows)
	Salt and fresh cracked pepper to taste
3	cups precooked pasta
	Parmesan cheese

Heat oil in a large sauté pan and lightly brown onion. Add venison and continue cooking until meat is cooked. Drain.

Add red wine and herbs, simmer until wine is nearly evaporated. Add tomato puree and juice and cook until mixture has the consistency of thick sauce (about 10 minutes).

Add roasted garlic by squeezing cooked cloves from the heads. Add cooked pasta and toss. Serve with Parmesan cheese.

Makes 4 servings.

ROASTED GARLIC:

Remove the tops of the fresh heads with a knife so that individual cloves of garlic are exposed; brush with olive oil.

Wrap in foil and bake at 350 degrees for one hour until cloves are golden.

98

CARAMELIZED GARLIC PHYLLO FOCACCIA

PRISCILLA YEE, Concord, CA

Keep extra phyllo in the freezer so you can make this easy appetizer any time you crave a "shot" of garlic.

Heat oven to 400 degrees. Place garlic cloves in greased 1 quart baking dish. Sprinkle thyme over top. Cover tightly with foil. Bake at 400 degrees for 30 minutes or until garlic is soft. Remove from oven.

Meanwhile, in a small bowl, combine oil and minced garlic.

Place 1 sheet phyllo on flat surface. Brush lightly with garlic oil and sprinkle with 1 tablespoon Parmesan. Repeat with remaining phyllo sheets, oil and Parmesan.

Place layered phyllo sheets, centered, in an ungreased 12-inch round pizza pan. Fold in excess dough at corners toward center, pleating as necessary to fit round shape of pan.

Layer mozzarella, red pepper, basil, tomatoes, and roasted garlic cloves over phyllo. Sprinkle with remaining Parmesan.

Bake on bottom rack of oven at 400 degrees for 15 to 20 minutes or until golden brown. Cool slightly before serving.

Garlic should be squeezed onto focaccia and peels discarded as you eat.

Makes 6 servings.

12	cloves fresh garlic, unpeeled
6	sprigs fresh thyme, 1 inch long
3	tablespoons olive oil
1	tablespoon minced fresh garlic
6	phyllo pastry sheets
½	cup grated Parmesan cheese
1	cup shredded mozzarella cheese
¼	teaspoon red pepper flakes
24	fresh basil leaves
4	Roma tomatoes, seeded, thinly sliced

The herb of mirth and medicine,
remedy and rancor
will be abundant in all its forms.

1991

THIRTEENTH ANNUAL GILROY GARLIC FESTIVAL

JULY · 26 · 27 · 28 · 1991

...*U*nder the pot lids of exciting ethnic cuisines
garlic has sneaked back into town.
The uppity little bulb is ever emerging
as the prime seasoning in favorite recipes.
Suddenly it's chic to reek.

TOWN AND COUNTRY

GARLIC PÂTÉ

ROSCOE PARKERSON, Slidell, LA

T̄his delectable hors d'oeuvre will impress guests at any gathering. The almonds add a rich and nutty flavor, complementing the pungency of the garlic. This pâté is one of the easiest-to-prepare we've ever seen!

Place garlic and almonds in food processor and puree. Add butter, olive oil, honey, and sea salt and process until smoothly blended.

Pack into a well-buttered rectangular pâté mold or small loaf pan and cover with foil. Place in a roasting pan and fill with boiling water to reach half way up sides of mold.

Bake for 1 hour at 350 degrees.

Uncover and bake for an additional hour.

Cool, cover tightly with plastic wrap and refrigerate overnight. Unmold by dipping mold in hot water.

Serve with country-style bread, toasted croutons or crackers.

Makes 20 servings.

2	pounds peeled fresh garlic cloves
1	oz. (2 tablespoons) blanched almonds
½	cup butter, softened
¼	cup extra virgin olive oil
1	teaspoon honey
½	teaspoon sea salt *or* kosher salt

GARLIC POLENTA HEARTS

GLORIA TOGNAZZINI, Santa Maria, CA

C̄apture the affections of those near to your heart with these prize-winning starters! A unique and delicious combination of polenta, aromatic Italian cheeses, and garlic creates a savory taste sensation the judges loved at first bite!

3	large heads fresh garlic, whole, unpeeled
1	14-oz. can chicken broth
1	cup coarse ground cornmeal or polenta
1	teaspoon salt
1	cup cold water
3	cups boiling water
½	cup (4–6 oz.) crumbled Gorgonzola cheese
½	cup grated Parmesan cheese
1	cup chopped red *or* green bell pepper, sautéed in olive oil until tender
1	cup dry Italian bread crumbs
1	egg mixed with 3 tablespoons water

Simmer garlic in chicken broth until easily pierced with a fork, about 20 minutes, turning once (add water if broth evaporates). Let cool, separate into cloves and peel.

Combine cornmeal with salt and cold water and very slowly add to large pot containing 3 cups boiling water, stirring constantly. Simmer, stirring often, for 30 to 40 minutes. Let cool slightly and stir in cheeses and bell pepper.

When cool enough to handle, pinch off a piece of polenta the size of a walnut, and with damp hands shape around a garlic clove. Roll in crumbs, then in egg mixture, and back in the crumbs. Place on a cookie sheet and repeat until polenta and garlic cloves are used up.

Preheat oven to 425 degrees and bake garlic polenta hearts for 20 minutes, or until light brown. Serve hot or at room temperature.

Makes approximately 50 appetizers.

101

CHICKEN MARGARITA

DONNA HOAG, Paso Robles, CA

A healthful and delicious way to bring the flavors of the southwest to your home. The refreshingly light marinade of lime and tequila makes this a perfect warm-weather supper—perhaps on the patio or deck?

Cut chicken into serving pieces and remove skin, or have this done by your butcher beforehand.

In a bowl, combine cumin, chile powder, lime juice, garlic, and 1 tablespoon of the olive oil. Marinate chicken pieces in this mixture for 20 minutes.

In a heavy skillet, heat remaining oil. Brown chicken pieces on all sides.

Add marinade, tequila, and water. Cover pan and poach gently until chicken is cooked through, about 25 minutes. Transfer chicken pieces to a platter.

Reduce sauce over high heat until of a good coating consistency and pour over chicken. Garnish with cilantro leaves.

Makes 4 servings.

Note: This dish goes well with rice, black beans, and a salad.

3	to 3½ lb. fresh frying chicken
1	tablespoon ground cumin
1	tablespoon chile powder
	Juice of 3 limes
10	cloves fresh garlic, finely chopped
3	tablespoons olive oil
½	cup tequila (white *or* gold)
½	cup water
1	bunch fresh cilantro for garnish

*O*nward garlic.
This innocent herb has staying power.
KANSAS CITY STAR

STUFFED SAUSAGE AND GARLIC ROLL

MARIE RIZZIO, Traverse City, MI

Here is a delectable variation of the stalwart English favorite, a Pig-in-a-Blanket.

1	16-oz. loaf frozen white bread dough
1	lb. bulk Italian sausage, crumbled
10	cloves fresh garlic, chopped fine
2	green onions, chopped
½	teaspoon salt
⅛	teaspoon ground black pepper
1	tablespoon fennel seeds
1	medium green bell pepper, chopped
2	ripe plum tomatoes, chopped
2	tablespoons fresh basil leaves, chopped
¼	cup grated Romano *or* Parmesan cheese
1	egg, beaten
1	tablespoon water
2	teaspoons sesame seeds
	Additional fresh basil sprigs for garnish

Place loaf of frozen dough in plastic bag. Let thaw overnight in refrigerator, or at room temperature for 2 hours. Cover and let dough rise until doubled in bulk.

Preheat oven to 350 degrees.

Brown sausage meat in a large skillet. Add garlic, green onion, salt, pepper, and fennel seeds, and cook for 2 minutes.

On floured surface, roll bread dough into a 10 × 12-inch rectangle and place on greased jelly roll pan.

Cover with sausage mixture in an even layer. Top with bell pepper, tomato, basil, and grated cheese. Roll up tightly, pinch edges shut and center in pan seam side down. Mix egg with water; brush over roll. Sprinkle with sesame seeds.

Bake for 40 to 45 minutes, or until golden brown. Let cool for 10 minutes before cutting into 1-inch thick diagonal slices. Overlap slices on serving platter and garnish with sprigs of basil.

Makes 6 to 8 servings.

103

GARLIC ON THE GRILL

LORETTA AHMED, Torrance, CA

You'll never grill ordinary hamburgers again after tasting these spicy prize-winners! The accompaniment of Hot Garlic Dip makes for a truly satisfying taste sensation. Time to break out the coals!

5   cloves fresh garlic
1   large onion, roughly chopped
2   lbs. lean ground beef
1   bunch fresh parsley, stems removed
1   bunch fresh cilantro, stems removed
1   tablespoon salt
1   tablespoon pepper
1   tablespoon cumin
1   tablespoon Tabasco sauce
    Pita bread pockets
    Hot Garlic Dip (recipe follows)

HOT GARLIC DIP:
4   cloves fresh garlic
1   medium onion, roughly chopped
3   tablespoons olive oil
5   small canned jalapeño chile peppers, drained
1   6-oz. can tomato paste
¼   cup water

Place garlic and onion in food processor and mince well. Transfer to mixing bowl and add ground beef, crumbling meat well.

Mince parsley and cilantro in food processor, and add to beef mixture. Sprinkle with salt, pepper, cumin, and Tabasco sauce, and mix well with your hands. Form into small patties and cook on hot grill to desired degree of doneness.

Place in pita pockets and serve with Hot Garlic Dip.

Makes 4 servings.

HOT GARLIC DIP:

Place garlic and onion in food processor and mince well.

Heat olive oil in a heavy skillet and add garlic, onion and jalapeño peppers. When onion is golden brown and softened, add tomato paste and enough water to make a dip consistency.

Makes approximately 1 cup.

104

ROSIE'S TERRIBLY SPICY RIBS

ROSE BURTCHBY, Ventura, CA

These ribs, inspired by the flavors of the Orient, will delight your friends and family as either a main dish or appetizer. Remember to plan ahead and let the meat marinate for a full 24 hours to allow the aromatic flavors of garlic, fresh ginger, and sesame to work their magic on these "Terribly Delicious" ribs!

1 rack (approximately 4 lbs.) lean pork ribs, cut into double rib sections.

MARINADE:
3 cloves fresh garlic, crushed
1 teaspoon minced fresh ginger root
½ cup soy sauce
½ cup honey
½ cup dry sherry
½ cup vermouth

COATING:
5 tablespoons minced fresh garlic
3 tablespoons minced fresh ginger root
2 tablespoons Oriental sesame oil
1 cup sesame seeds, divided
1 cup finely chopped fresh cilantro, divided

In a glass or stainless steel bowl, combine marinade ingredients. Add ribs and turn to coat. Cover with plastic wrap and marinate in refrigerator for 24 hours or longer, turning occasionally.

Preheat oven to 325 degrees.

Remove ribs from marinade and pat semi-dry. Combine coating mixture of garlic, ginger and sesame oil, and rub into meat. Combine half cup of sesame seeds with half cup of cilantro and roll ribs into this mixture. Bake for 20 minutes.

Turn ribs, sprinkle with half the remaining cilantro and sesame seeds, and bake for a further 20 minutes.

Turn ribs, sprinkle with remaining cilantro and sesame seeds, and bake for 15 minutes more or until tender.

Makes 4 servings as a main dish, or 8 as an appetizer cut into single rib pieces.

MORE THAN A TOUCH OF CLASS RICE

ALMA CAREY, Hot Springs, AR

Tired of the usual rice or potatoes dilemma? This aromatic and truly elegant savory rice accompaniment will jazz up any main dish, and bring a unique "touch of class" to any table.

2	heads fresh garlic
	Olive oil
3	cups cooked brown rice, warm
¼	cup butter *or* margarine, melted
½	cup dairy sour cream
½	cup heavy cream, whipped
	Salt

Preheat oven to 325 degrees.

Rub heads of garlic with olive oil, wrap loosely in foil and place on baking sheet. Bake for 1¼ to 1½ hours. Garlic will be properly roasted when it is lightly browned, softened and smells deliciously sweet.

Squeeze pulp from skins and stir into warm rice. Add butter, sour cream and whipped cream. Stir to blend. Season with salt to taste. May be served at room temperature or chilled.

Makes 6 to 8 servings.

GARLIC AND CHILE RELLENO SOUFFLE

MARIA SANDOVAL, Alameda, CA

A new take on a traditional Mexican dish! This relleno casserole is a real time-saver, yet captures the true essence of this delightful dish of old Mexico.

Preheat oven to 375 degrees.

Grease a 1½ quart souffle mold or Pyrex baking dish generously with butter, and dust well with bread crumbs. Set aside.

Heat 3 tablespoons of the butter until it foams, add flour, and cook over medium heat until it starts to brown, stirring constantly. Add hot milk and cook for 4 minutes, stirring constantly, until thickened. Season with ¼ teaspoon of the salt, and white pepper. Let cool slightly and add the beaten egg yolks, then the chiles, and mix well.

Sauté garlic in remaining 2 tablespoons butter until golden brown. Add to the above mixture.

Beat egg whites with a pinch of salt until stiff. Fold beaten egg whites into first mixture; then fold in the grated cheese.

Pour into prepared mold and bake for 35 to 40 minutes, until puffed and brown.

Makes 4 to 6 servings.

106

	Softened butter and dry bread crumbs for mold
5	tablespoons butter, softened
3	tablespoons all-purpose flour
1	cup hot milk
¼	teaspoon plus 1 pinch salt
⅛	teaspoon white pepper
4	large egg yolks, well beaten
17	oz. can peeled green chiles, drained and patted dry, cut in 1-inch pieces
8	cloves fresh garlic, minced
5	large egg whites
½	cup grated Monterey Jack cheese

GARLIC BASIL BREAD PUDDING

KAREN DAVIS, Oklahoma City, OK

This is a wonderful substitute for Yorkshire pudding served with a standing ribbed roast, or any other kind of roast for that matter. Puddings can also be served for brunch with a green salad.

2	cups half-and-half
10	cloves fresh garlic, chopped
3	large eggs
2	tablespoons minced fresh parsley
2	tablespoons minced fresh basil
¾	teaspoon salt
	Black pepper to taste
2½	cups sourdough bread cubes (½ inch cubes), without crust
	Parmesan cheese
	Basil sprigs for garnish

In a heavy saucepan, scald half-and-half with garlic. Remove from heat and let stand for 15 minutes to infuse garlic. Strain mixture and discard solids.

In a bowl, beat eggs and add lukewarm half-and-half in a stream, stirring constantly. Stir in parsley, basil, salt, and pepper to taste.

Divide bread cubes among 8 well-buttered muffin cups. Ladle the custard mixture evenly in the muffin cups. Let stand for 10 minutes so bread can absorb liquid.

Preheat oven to 350 degrees.

Sprinkle tops of puddings with Parmesan cheese and bake for 45 minutes, or until golden brown and puffed. Remove muffin pan from oven and let stand for 10 minutes.

Run a thin knife blade around the sides of each pudding and lift out carefully with a fork. Serve warm, garnished with basil sprigs.

Makes 4 to 8 servings.

Note: If baking in mini-muffin pans to serve as an appetizer, reduce baking time to 25 to 30 minutes.

JO-C'S GARLIC BREAD STICKS

JOSEPHINE CAMPISI, Mashpee, MA

These aromatic bread sticks are the perfect hors d'oeuvre for a cocktail party, and you'll want to keep a tin of them on hand for snacking.

20	cloves fresh garlic, peeled and roughly chopped
1¼	cups olive oil
1	package dry yeast
1	teaspoon sugar
¾	cup water, warm
6	cups all-purpose flour
1	tablespoon ground black pepper
1	tablespoon salt
2	tablespoons fennel *or* anise seeds
7	oz. beer, at room temperature

Place garlic and ¼ cup of the olive oil in food processor or blender and puree. Add remaining oil and set aside.

Mix together yeast, sugar, and warm water. Let stand for 10 minutes, until foamy.

In a large bowl, combine flour, pepper, salt, and fennel seeds. Make a well in the center, and add garlic oil mixture, yeast mixture and beer. Mix together until it forms a ball.

Let dough rest for 15 minutes, then knead on a lightly floured surface for 1 minute and let rest again. Repeat this process three times. Pinch off small pieces of dough and roll into 5- to 6-inch slender sausage shapes. Place on ungreased cookie sheets.

Preheat oven to 375 degrees. Bake for 20 to 25 minutes, until light golden brown.

Makes about 90 bread sticks.

GARLICKY FLORENTINE PESTO MUFFINS

CHRISTINE SIMS, Hayward, CA

The judges were wowed by Christine's savory mini muffins. They'll add a winning "bite" to your Sunday brunch.

3	cups all-purpose flour
1	teaspoon salt (optional)
1½	teaspoons baking soda
¾	teaspoon baking powder
3	large eggs
1	cup milk
1	cup vegetable oil
1	package (10 oz.) frozen chopped spinach, thawed and squeezed dry
2	teaspoons fines herbes
½	cup pesto sauce
1	cup grated Monterey Jack cheese
¼	cup minced fresh garlic

Preheat oven to 375 degrees.

Spray mini-muffin plaque with vegetable coating.

Sift flour, salt, soda, and baking powder together. Beat eggs with milk and add to flour mixture. Stir in oil and spinach and mix well. Fold in fines herbes, pesto, grated cheese, and garlic.

Spoon into muffin cups and bake for 12 to 15 minutes, until nicely browned.

Makes 18.

108

GARLIC THREE BEAN BREAD

JIM KELLY, La Canada, CA

Three beans in bread? The addition of legumes and fresh herbs to whole wheat bread constituted a winner. Try it toasted with cream cheese and lox instead of a bagel.

Peel and chop garlic and onion. Heat 3 tablespoons of the olive oil in a heavy skillet and sauté garlic and onion until light gold. Set aside to cool.

In a large bowl, or in electric mixer with dough hook attached, dissolve yeast in beer. Add honey. Stir in 2 cups whole wheat flour and 1 cup bread flour. Mix until uniform, then set aside for 30 to 60 minutes, until bubbles form.

Add garlic and onion mixture, beans, parsley, basil, oregano, vinegar, and salt. Mix well. Add remaining flour, half cup at a time, until a dough is formed. At this point, the dough should clean the sides of the bowl (if mixing by hand, turn out onto a lightly floured surface and knead for 5 minutes).

Grease bowl with olive oil and add ball of dough, turning to coat all sides. Cover with plastic wrap. Let rise until doubled in bulk, about 1 hour.

Punch dough down and divide into 4 or 6 parts. Form each into a ball. Place on two oiled baking sheets, seam side down. Cover and let rise until doubled in bulk, about 1 hour.

Preheat oven to 375 degrees.

Brush tops of loaves with beaten egg. Slash top surfaces 2 or 3 times with a sharp knife, perhaps with your initial.

Bake for 25 to 35 minutes, until center reaches 190 degrees or until golden brown. Let cool on racks.

Makes 4 to 6 loaves.

1	head fresh garlic
1	large red onion
4	tablespoons extra virgin olive oil
1	package active dry yeast
2¼	cups beer, gently heated
⅓	cup honey
2	cups whole wheat flour
4	cups bread flour
1	cup cooked *or* canned black beans, drained
1	cup cooked *or* canned red kidney beans, drained
1	cup cooked *or* canned garbanzo beans (chick peas), drained
¼	cup chopped fresh parsley
¼	cup chopped fresh basil
⅛	cup chopped fresh *or* 1 tablespoon dried oregano
½	teaspoon tarragon vinegar
2	teaspoons salt
1	beaten egg for glaze

1992

Mary
Harsh

Gilroy Garlic Festival
July 24, 25, 26, 1992

Gilroy, California. Population 20,000.
Except in early August. Then it swells fivefold.
One hundred thousand people going bananas over GARLIC!

TWA AMBASSADOR MAGAZINE

GARLIC MUSHROOM SOUP

J. O. MANIS, Mill Valley, CA

*Ordinary ingredients made extraordinarily good in their combination.
You can whip this tasty soup up in less than 30 minutes.*

20	cloves fresh garlic, peeled
1½	lbs. fresh mushrooms
4	tablespoons olive oil
2	cups toasted bread crumbs
1	bunch fresh parsley, stems removed, chopped fine
10	cups fresh *or* canned chicken broth
	Salt and pepper to taste
	Dash Tabasco
	Dry sherry wine to taste (optional)

In a food processor or by hand, finely chop garlic and 1 pound of the mushrooms. Cut remaining mushrooms into thin slices.

In a 4 quart saucepan, heat 2 tablespoons of the olive oil and sauté garlic and mushrooms for 3 minutes. Remove from pan and set aside.

Sauté bread crumbs in remaining oil. Add garlic and mushroom mixture to crumbs, stir in parsley, and sauté for 5 minutes. Add broth and simmer, stirring frequently, for 15 minutes. Season to taste with salt, pepper, Tabasco, and dry sherry if desired.

Makes 8 to 10 servings.

Note: If a thicker soup is desired, stir in a few teaspoons of cornstarch dissolved in a little cold water and simmer for a few minutes until soup clears and thickens.

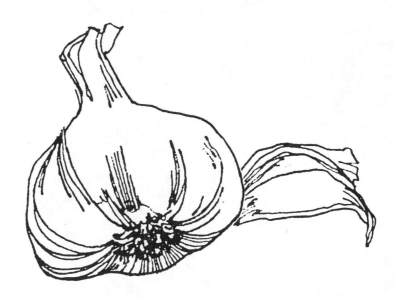

111

CALIFORNIA GARLIC AND CHICKEN ROLL UPS

ROXANNE E. CHAN, Albany, CA

Here's another winner from perennial finalist, Roxanne Chan. We think the fragrant chicken rolls are a perfect addition to a Sunday brunch buffet.

2	heads fresh garlic
1	tablespoon vegetable oil
2	oz. fresh soft goat cheese
8	chicken breast halves, boned and skinned
1	cup shredded raw spinach
4	tablespoons diced roasted red bell pepper
¼	cup olive oil
3	cloves fresh garlic, pressed (for basting mixture)
1	tablespoon balsamic vinegar
½	teaspoon ground black pepper
1	tablespoon capers, drained
1	tablespoon dried currants, rinsed and drained
1	tablespoon sliced almonds
1	small green onion, minced
1	tablespoon minced fresh basil
	Basil sprigs for garnish

Preheat oven to 350 degrees.

Cut garlic heads crosswise in two, about ⅓ from root end. Place vegetable oil in an 8-inch baking dish. Add garlic, cut side down. Bake until cloves are very soft, about 1 hour. When cool enough to handle, squeeze garlic pulp into a small bowl. Add goat cheese and mix well.

Place chicken breasts between two sheets of plastic wrap and pound to ⅛-inch thickness.

Spread garlic mixture on the breasts. Top with spinach and bell peppers. Roll up to enclose filling and secure with wooden toothpick if needed.

Combine olive oil, pressed garlic, vinegar, and black pepper. Brush the roll-ups.

Broil 4 inches from heat for 5 minutes. Turn, brush again and broil 5 minutes more or until chicken is tender. Brush once more, slice, and arrange on a platter.

Combine remaining basting mixture with capers, currants, almonds, green onions, and minced basil. Spoon over sliced roll-ups and garnish dish with basil sprigs.

Makes 6 to 8 servings.

OVEN BAKED PORTUGUESE RIBS WITH GARLIC

KAREN VIVEIROS, Sunnyvale, CA

This is a traditional family recipe. Often the meat is left to marinate for 2 to 3 days, imparting a wonderful flavor. Serve this dish with green salad and Portuguese sweet bread.

26	cloves fresh garlic, peeled
2	tablespoons salt
6	whole cloves, crushed
6	allspice berries, crushed
2	bay leaves, crumbled
2	teaspoons paprika
2	teaspoons cayenne pepper
1	cup dry red wine
1	cup water
1	lemon, sliced
4	lbs. thick country-style spareribs, cut in serving size pieces.

Crush 6 garlic cloves with the salt in a mortar, or with the flat of a knife on a board. Transfer paste to a bowl and work in the cloves, allspice, bay leaves, paprika, cayenne pepper, wine, and water. Add lemon slices.

Place ribs in a shallow dish and add marinade, turning ribs to make sure that all are coated. Marinate for at least 2 hours, and preferably longer.

Preheat oven to 350 degrees.

Remove ribs from marinade and place in a shallow baking dish. Add the remaining 20 cloves of garlic and 1 cup of marinade to the pan.

Cover and bake for 1½ hours or until tender, basting every 30 minutes. Bake uncovered for the final 30 minutes.

Makes 4 to 6 servings.

113

THE ONLY B.B.Q. SALMON

DAVID and PAT VELJACIC, Coquitlam, B.C. Canada

Instead of marinating and grilling, slow cooking in a covered barbeque infused the fish with the flavors of the garlic and seasonings. This version of barbequed salmon stood out among the entries in 1992.

10	large fresh garlic cloves, peeled
1	teaspoon salt
¼	cup olive oil
4	tablespoons finely chopped fresh parsley
1½	tablespoons minced sun dried tomatoes in olive oil
1	3 to 4 lb. salmon fillet, deboned (Sockeye, Coho or Spring)
	Fresh green lettuce leaves

A day ahead, crush the garlic cloves with the flat of a wide blade knife, and then chop. Pour salt on top and mash into the garlic. Combine garlic, olive oil, parsley and sun dried tomatoes in a covered jar. Let stand overnight in refrigerator.

When ready to prepare salmon, cut two lengthwise slits in the fillet with a sharp knife, dividing the surface of the fish into thirds. Cut to the skin, but not through it. Spread half the garlic mixture over the fillet, pressing into the slits.

Place salmon on grill, skin side down, over low heat in covered barbecue. Close lid and cook for 15 minutes. Spread remaining garlic mixture over fillet. Close lid, increase heat to medium and cook for another 15 minutes. Test fish for doneness.

Remove fish from grill by inserting spatulas between the skin and the flesh, lifting the fillet but leaving the skin on the grill. Place the skinless and boneless fillet on a bed of fresh green lettuce leaves.

Makes 6 to 8 servings.

114

PASTA SAPORTIA

KAREN NICHOLES McVARISH, Davis, CA

Karen McVarish, who submitted this fresh-tasting, pungent pasta dish, suggests serving it with a salad of fresh sliced vine-ripened tomatoes.

4	to 5 heads fresh garlic, separated into cloves, peeled and sliced ⅛ inch wide (like slivered almonds) to make about 2 cups
4½	cups dry sherry wine
1½	teaspoons salt
1	pound large pasta shells
1	tablespoon butter *or* margarine
1¼	cups Parmesan cheese, freshly grated
1	teaspoon olive oil
5	shallots, thinly sliced
6	cups fresh basil leaves, loosely packed
1	cup heavy cream
	Fresh ground black pepper

FRESH GARLIC AND BASIL PASTA:

Place garlic slivers and sherry in medium large saucepan. Over high heat, boil down until only enough sherry remains to barely cover the garlic slivers (about 1¼ cups), this should take 10 to 15 minutes. Reduce heat to low, cover pot with tight-fitting lid and cook slowly for about 45 minutes. Do not allow to boil dry.

While garlic is cooking, bring to a boil 4 quarts of water with one teaspoon salt in a large pot, and add pasta. Cook, stirring occasionally to prevent sticking, until *al dente*, about 12 to 14 minutes.

Drain well and stir in butter, sprinkle with remaining salt and ½ cup Parmesan. Mix well.

After garlic is cooked, there should be a little less than a cup of liquid left. It there is more, boil uncovered to reduce.

Heat olive oil in large skillet over medium high heat. Add shallots and cook, stirring for 45 seconds. Add garlic and sherry mixture. Bring to a hard boil over high heat and add basil. Simmer gently just until wilted (about 60 seconds). Stir in cream and a grinding of black pepper. Continue simmering sauce until it thickens slightly, about 2 minutes.

Pour sauce over pasta and mix well. Stir in remaining Parmesan, retaining 2 tablespoons for garnish. Transfer to a heated serving bowl or individual plates, and sprinkle with Parmesan.

Makes 6 to 8 servings.

115

GILROY CONFETTI

NELLY STARK, Rocklin, CA

A garlicky take on a middle-eastern favorite, couscous, this dish makes an excellent vegetarian main dish (substituting feta cheese for the prosciutto). Or bring it along to your next potluck barbeque.

18	cloves fresh garlic, peeled
¼	cup chopped prosciutto
2	teaspoons Dijon mustard
	Juice of 1 lemon
2	teaspoons rice wine vinegar
4	tablespoons plus 2 teaspoons peanut oil *or* walnut oil
	Dash dried hot red pepper flakes
2½	cups chicken broth
2	cups couscous (*or* bulgur, follow package directions for cooking)
¼	cup finely diced red bell pepper
¼	cup finely diced green bell pepper
¼	cup finely diced celery
¼	cup finely diced carrot
½	cup pine nuts, toasted (*or* peanuts, toasted and chopped)
	Strips of prosciutto and lemon peel for garnish

In a small skillet, sauté garlic and prosciutto over medium high heat until garlic is softened but not mushy.

Reserve 5 garlic cloves for garnish.

Transfer remaining garlic and prosciutto to food processor or blender. Add mustard, lemon juice, vinegar, 4 tablespoons oil, and red pepper flakes. Mix well to make dressing and reserve.

In a 2-quart pan, bring chicken broth and remaining oil to a boil. Add couscous, mix gently cover and remove from heat. Let stand for 15 to 30 minutes. Fluff with a fork and let cool uncovered for a few minutes.

In a medium bowl, combine red and green bell pepper, celery, carrots, and pine nuts. Add couscous and gently mix to combine. Add dressing and mix well.

Garnish with reserved garlic cloves, prosciutto strips, and lemon peel strips. Serve immediately or refrigerate, but bring to room temperature before serving.

Makes 8 servings.

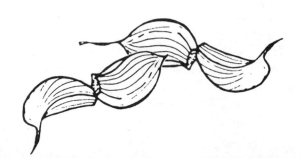

LUSCIOUS GARLICKY YORKSHIRE PUDDING

AUSBERTO SANDOVAL, Santa Rosa, CA

This wonderful Yorkshire pudding recipe is bound to become a tradition at your holiday table.

3	cups milk
2	cups flour
	Salt and pepper
3	eggs, beaten
6	slices bacon
10	cloves fresh garlic, peeled and chopped fine

Whisk together milk and flour until no lumps remain. Season with salt and pepper to taste. Add eggs and mix well. Let rest for 30 minutes.

Meanwhile, fry bacon until crisp. Remove with slotted spoon, drain on paper towels, and crumble.

Preheat oven to 400 degrees.

Sauté garlic in bacon fat until golden. Be careful not to burn. Remove with slotted spoon and drain on paper towels.

Place 3 tablespoons of the bacon fat in a 9 × 13 inch baking dish and put in the oven to get really hot.

Add crumbled bacon and sautéed garlic to flour mixture and stir lightly to mix.

Holding hot baking dish with an oven mitt, tilt to coat the inside with bacon drippings. Pour in flour mixture.

Bake for 20 minutes, then reduce heat to 350 degrees. Bake for a further 15 minutes, until pudding is puffed and brown. Cut in squares to serve.

Use as an accompaniment to roasts, chops, etc.

Makes 6 servings.

117

No one is indifferent to garlic. People either love it or hate it, and most good cooks seem to belong to the first group.

FAYE LEVY

1993

GILROY
GARLIC FESTIVAL

JULY 23, 24, 25, 1993

SILVER BILL'S GARBAÑERO TONGUETWISTER

BILL MAXWELL, Vandalia, MO

Most garlicky recipe.

1	quart peeled garlic cloves
6	to 12 bright red habañero peppers
2	6-ounce bottles Goya Hot Sauce
1	tablespoon seasoned salt
1	tablespoon freshly ground black pepper

Snip the cluster end off each garlic clove. Remove seeds from the habañero peppers. Use at least six habañeros, or more, depending upon their size and the maker's taste.

Combine all ingredients and liquefy in a blender. For a thinner sauce add more Goya Hot Sauce.

A half cup of Silver Bill's Garbañero Tonguetwister is rumored to be capable of reviving a horse that's been dead less than an hour.

SUMMERTIME GARLIC PENNE

SARAH WALKER, Venice, CA

Roasting the bell peppers adds an especially rich, smokey flavor to this already hearty dish.

3	red bell peppers
	Salt
1/3	cup plus 1 teaspoon olive oil
1	lb. penne, or other tube-shaped pasta
6	large cloves fresh garlic, peeled and minced
8	ounces feta cheese, at room temperature, crumbled
1/2	cup shredded fresh basil leaves
	Freshly milled black pepper

Halve, core and seed peppers. Roast or broil until skins start to blister and blacken. When cool enough to handle, pull off papery skin. Cut into thick strips about 1½ inches long and set aside. Bring a large pot of water to a boil and add ½ teaspoon salt and 1 teaspoon olive oil, to prevent pasta from sticking. Add penne and cook until tender but still firm. Meanwhile, heat remaining olive oil in a skillet and sauté garlic until it turns golden. Drain pasta and place in a large, shallow, heated bowl. Add garlic and olive oil and toss well. Add feta, pepper strips, and basil. Season to taste with salt and pepper, and toss again to mix.

Makes 4 servings.

119

GILROY MARINATED SHRIMP SALADE

JESSIE LYN ANDERSON, Evanston, IL

A fresh (and refreshing) approach to shrimp salad—guaranteed to be a new summer favorite.

1	whole head garlic
	Olive oil
⅔	cup mayonnaise
⅔	cup sour half and half (*or* light sour cream)
1	clove garlic, minced
¼	cup chile sauce
1½	teaspoon fresh lemon juice
½	teaspoon prepared horseradish
1	pound shrimp, cooked and cleaned
	Assortment of lettuce and greens
	Lemon wedges for garnish

Preheat oven to 350. Peel off outer layers of skin on garlic head and cut ends off one side to expose cloves. Rub with olive oil and wrap in foil. Bake for 20–25 minutes until tender. Squeeze cloves into work bowl of food processor. Process to form paste. Add remaining ingredients except shrimp and mixed greens. Process with on and off turn to blend. Place shrimp in non-metallic bowl. Pour sauce over. Cover and refrigerate overnight (or at least 6 hours). Divide greens among 4 or 5 individual serving plates. Spoon equal amounts of shrimp mixture over each and garnish with lemon wedges.

Serves 4–5.

*G*arlic is the king of seasonings.

DONNA SEGAL
INDIANAPOLIS STAR

SPICY GRILLED RACK OF LAMB WITH A GARLICKY HOKITIKA MARINADE

RICHARD G. ROSIVACH, Syracuse, NY

The marinade gives this traditional rack of lamb an exotic, oriental flavor.

1	cup 1991 Sauvignon Blanc
¼	cup White Wine Worcestershire
½	teaspoon wasabi powder
3	cloves fresh garlic, chopped
2	tablespoons fresh rosemary, chopped
5	tablespoons fresh squeezed lime juice
¼	teaspoon salt
¼	teaspoon fresh ground pepper
4	New Zealand racks of lamb, 9 oz. each

Combine all ingredients except the lamb in a small bowl and whisk thoroughly.

Cut racks of lamb vertically along the bone to make segments about ½ inch each.

Place lamb segments in a large zip-lock bag and pour in the marinade.

Seal bag tightly and shake until thoroughly coated.

Place bag in a shallow pan and refrigerate 24 hours.

Pour entire mixture into a small colander and discard the liquid.

Grill lamb over high heat for approximately 2 minutes on each side.

Serve immediately with a small salad and a light vinaigrette.

Serves 4.

GARLIC HEAVEN TURKEY

LINDA ZWEIG, San Diego, CA

You don't need gravy—it's so moist!!!!!!!!!

1	turkey, whole, 18 to 22 lbs.
½	cup extra virgin olive oil
½	cup Cribari marsala wine
2	lbs. *fresh* garlic—cloves separated and peeled
2	tablespoons coarse salt
1	tablespoon fresh cracked black pepper
1	tablespoon fresh oregano
1	tablespoon fresh rosemary
	Salt and pepper to taste
	Olive oil
	Extra marsala

Preheat oven to 400 degrees.

Rinse and clean turkey and discard fat.

Using a food processor with chopping blade attached, pour in olive oil and marsala wine.

Add peeled garlic cloves, one handful at a time, using on/off turns until chopped medium fine.

Add salt, pepper, oregano, and rosemary. Mix using 3 short on/off turns. Scrape mixture into small bowl and set aside.

Grease bottom and sides of roasting pan with olive oil.

Place turkey into prepared pan. Carefully separate skin from breast down to and around the legs, leaving skin at center of breast bone attached. Lift flap of skin at rear of turkey. Using a small knife, make an incision from left to right approximately 3 inches deep and 4 to 6 inches across.

Stuff a handful of Garlic Heaven into pocket. Take skin flap and fold under turkey.

Stuff Garlic Heaven a little at a time under skin covering the entire side of the breast to the thigh and leg. Repeat on other side.

Coat inside of turkey cavity with Garlic Heaven.

With remaining Garlic Heaven coat entire surface of turkey including legs and wings.

Salt and pepper entire surface to taste.

Pour ¼ cup marsala wine into turkey cavity and the rest into roasting pan.

Cover. (If lid touches top of turkey, use heavy-duty foil. Make sure foil is sealed around entire pan and does not touch top of turkey.) Place in preheated oven and bake at 400 for 1½ hours.

Remove from oven and reduce heat to 375 degrees. *Carefully* remove lid or foil.

Baste turkey, being careful not to wash off Garlic Heaven.

Return to oven for 25 minutes. Baste 3–4 more times. (If Garlic Heaven looks like it's burning turn oven down to 350.)

Turkey should be loose on the bone.

MARISCOS A LA CALIFORNIA

ELIZABETH R. NORRIS, Oakland, CA

This recipe combines Spanish flavor with California fresh and healthy. If you want to eat this Spanish style, you drizzle olive oil over it before eating. Buen provecho!

3	tablespoons extra light olive oil
5	cloves garlic, crushed lightly, thinly sliced crosswise
2	small potatoes, scrubbed, not peeled
1	small Spanish onion, thinly sliced
2	medium tomatoes, diced with seeds removed
½	lb. scallops
½	lb. prawns, peeled and deveined
1	small green bell pepper, cut into strips
1	small red bell pepper, cut into strips
1	small yellow bell pepper, cut into strips
	Garlic salt and lemon pepper
	Butter lettuce
	Lemon wedges

Prepare all ingredients before cooking. In a large skillet fry garlic in olive oil until light brown, remove and discard. Fry potatoes and onions until translucent. Add tomatoes; cover and cook over medium heat 5 minutes or until potatoes look cooked. Add scallops and prawns and sauté until scallops whiten and prawns turn red. Add peppers; season to taste with garlic salt and lemon pepper. Remove from heat when peppers are done but not wilted.

Serve on a bed of butter lettuce. Garnish with lemon wedges. Serve with garlic bread.

Makes 4 servings.

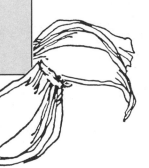

123

SHRIMP PERLU

DAVID and PAT VELJACIC, Coquitlam, B.C., Canada

The unusual combination of flavors makes this a particularly piquant dish.

10	large garlic cloves, minced
4	tablespoons olive oil
1	cup celery hearts, chopped
½	cup red bell peppers, chopped
2	cups large shrimp, shelled and deveined
1	large Italian sausage, cooked and chopped in ¼-inch pieces
5	large garlic cloves, slivered
2	to 4 tablespoons sweet hot sauce (Tiger Sauce)
1	tablespoon black pepper (Tellicherry)
	Salt to taste
4	cups cooked rice, cooled

In a large fry pan sauté the minced garlic for five minutes in the olive oil, over a low heat. DO NOT BURN....

Add the celery heart and bell pepper and sauté over a low heat until the vegetables just start to turn limp.

Add the shrimp and Italian sausage, sauté until the shrimp is cooked (about 3 minutes). Stir in the slivered garlic, hot sauce, and black pepper.

Salt to taste.

Add the rice, mix in well and cook until the entire dish is hot, stirring often.

Serves 4.

ODORIFEROUS PUNGENT CATFISH

BARBARA J. MORGAN, Concord, CA

The title says it all!

Mash the garlic in the salt. Coarsely chop two of the long green chiles and set them aside. Sauté the garlic, onion, jalapeño peppers, and cilantro in 2 tablespoons butter over low heat until tender. Add tomato, chopped chiles, and sugar to the onion mixture and cook, stirring 3 minutes. Set the sauce aside.

Char the remaining 4 long green chiles under the broiler, turning them frequently. Peel the chiles, split, seed, and chop, adding to the sauce.

Melt butter in skillet and when hot, sauté catfish for 1 to 2 minutes on each side. Quickly transfer to a platter and spoon sauce over top. Serve with rice.

Serves 4.

124

8	cloves garlic
1	teaspoon salt
6	long green chiles
½	cup sliced onion
2	fresh jalapeño peppers, seeded and sliced
1	tablespoon minced fresh cilantro
2	tablespoons butter
1	tomato, cored and diced
	Dash of sugar
4	catfish fillets
2	tablespoons butter

BEDONI'S GARLICKY OYSTER BOAT

JOHN D. BEDONI, Rocklin, CA

This makes a delightful and delicious centerpiece for buffet entertaining.

1	1-lb. loaf sourdough French bread
55	cloves fresh garlic, peeled
4	tablespoons olive oil
8	thick strips bacon
1	large yellow onion, finely chopped
½	cup seasoned dry breadcrumbs
1½	cups grated Parmesan cheese
7	large eggs
10	medium oysters, shucked
½	cup heavy cream

Cut top from loaf, leaving sides intact. Scoop out white crumbs to form a boat shape. Place hollow loaf on cookie sheet under broiler and toast lightly. Remove and set aside. Preheat oven to 350 degrees. Toss garlic cloves with olive oil and spread on cookie sheet. Bake for 30 minutes, turning cloves after 15 minutes, and reserve. In a dry skillet, cook bacon until done. Remove and drain on paper towels. Pour off all but 2 tablespoons of bacon fat and drippings, reserving remainder for oysters. Add chopped onion to skillet; sauté until golden. Remove with slotted spoon and reserve. In a small bowl, combine dry breadcrumbs with ½ cup of the Parmesan cheese. In a second bowl, beat 2 of the eggs. Add reserved bacon fat to skillet and heat. Pat oysters dry on paper towels. Dip in egg, then in crumb mixture, add to skillet and sauté until lightly browned. In a large bowl, beat remaining 5 eggs. Add sautéed onion and cream and mix well. Crumble bacon over this mixture and stir in. Lay roasted garlic cloves in bottom loaf and smash with a fork. Top with oysters. Pour egg mixture over oysters and sprinkle with remaining Parmesan. Bake for 1 hour. Cut into slices and serve hot or at room temperature.

Makes 6 to 8 servings.

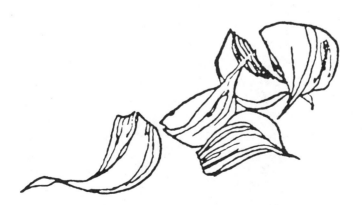

125

SHELLFISH IN GARLIC-SAFFRON BROTH

KAREN VIVEIROS, Sunnyvale, CA

The idea for this recipe came from a favorite garlic cream soup recipe and San Francisco-style Cioppino recipe. Add a touch of saffron and it makes a delicious soup.

12	small fresh clams, scrubbed
12	fresh mussels, cleaned
1½ cups	dry white wine (reserve 1 cup for the broth)
30	garlic cloves
3 tablespoons	olive oil
1	carrot, cut into julienne strips
½ cup	julienne red bell pepper strips
3 cups	chicken broth
½ teaspoon	crumbled saffron threads
8	medium shrimp, shelled and deveined
8	scallops
1 tablespoon	chopped fresh cilantro, plus 4 sprigs for garnish

In large covered saucepan, over moderately high heat, steam the clams and the mussels with ½ cup wine, shaking the pan occasionally, for 5 to 6 minutes, or until the clams and mussels have opened. Discard any unopened shells. Remove 4 clams and 4 mussels in their shells for garnish. Remove the remaining clams and mussels from their shells and reserve them in a small bowl. Discard the cooking liquid.

Crush the garlic into a coarse paste. In the saucepan over moderately low heat, cook the garlic paste, the carrot, and the bell pepper in the oil, stirring, for 10 minutes, or until the vegetables are tender and the garlic is just beginning to color. Stir in the broth, the remaining 1 cup of wine, and the saffron, and bring to a boil. Simmer for 30 minutes. Add the shrimp and the scallops, simmer the mixture for 2 to 3 minutes, or until the shrimp are pink, stir in the reserved shelled clams and mussels, and the chopped cilantro. Ladle the mixture into bowls, garnish it with the reserved clams and mussels in their shells and a sprig of cilantro, and serve it with sourdough french bread toasts.

Serves 4.

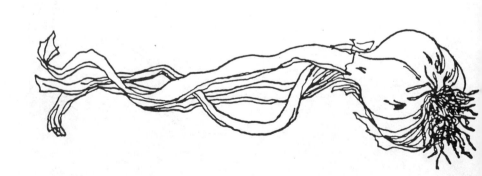

RATATOUILLE A LA GARLIQUE

RONI GEHLKE, Antioch, CA

This dish, which originates from southern France but also works well with California-grown garlic, provides a zesty, festy combination of fresh garden veggies, herbs, and garlic, garlic, garlic.

½ cup olive oil

2 large eggplants, cubed

6 zucchinis, cubed

2 large onions, sliced

3 green peppers, sliced

2 red peppers, sliced

1 small bunch of celery, sliced

9 ounces chopped garlic (very important!)

6 tomatoes, peeled and seeded, sliced thickly

2 sticks cinnamon

½ teaspoon garlic salt

1 teaspoon *each* of dried oregano, basil, and thyme leaves

Freshly ground black pepper

2 tablespoons sugar

1 tablespoon Worcestershire sauce

1 teaspoon Mrs. Dash *or* salt substitute

2 tablespoons red hot sauce

3 tablespoons red wine vinegar

Parsley (optional)

Grated Parmesan cheese

Open jar of chopped garlic and inhale deeply. This will put you in the proper mood for cooking.

In a large heavy pot, heat the olive oil. Over medium-high heat, sauté the eggplant, zucchini, onion, pepper, celery, and other sundry garden delights with 6 ounces of garlic until vegetables are heated thoroughly and glisten. Set aside remaining garlic.

Add tomatoes, cinnamon, garlic salt, herbs, black pepper, sugar, Worcestershire sauce, Mrs. Dash, and red hot sauce.

Partially cover the pot and cook over low heat for 2 hours or until liquid is reduced and zesty flavors are combined. Rent a movie. Add the wine vinegar in the last 15 minutes. What the heck, toss in some more garlic too.

Taste and adjust seasonings to desired flavor. Finished dish should have a pungent sweet and sour taste. If not, mix in some more garlic.

Pour into a bowl and decorate with parsley and sliced red peppers. Serve hot over steamed white rice as a tasty main dish. Sprinkle hot sauce and Parmesan cheese on top to add additional flavor. May also be chilled and served cold.

Makes 3 quarts.

127

POLENTA CON BACI DA GILROY

PATRICIA C. TRINCHERO, Gilroy, CA

Polenta with kisses from Gilroy.

1	ounce Porcini mushrooms dried (Italian dried mushrooms)
1	cup water
2	heads garlic
½	cup parsley, chopped fine
4	to 5 large shiitake mushrooms
1	small red bell pepper, julienned
½	lb. block of Jack cheese
3	tablespoons olive oil
1	tablespoon coarse oregano
	Salt and pepper to taste
4	cups water
½	teaspoon salt
1	cup polenta meal
1	tablespoon butter *or* margarine

Soak dried Porcini mushrooms in 1 cup water about one hour before use. Clean and peel garlic heads then slice each clove into 2 or 3 thick slivers. Wash and clean parsley, quarter the shiitakes, julienne the red pepper and set aside. Slice the Jack cheese into ⅛-inch thick slices and set aside.

Heat the olive oil over low heat and add all the garlic. Sprinkle the oregano over the garlic and salt and pepper to taste. Slowly simmer for approximately 30 minutes using low heat.

While garlic is cooking, heat 4 cups of water to boiling in a double boiler. Add ½ teaspoon salt to the water. When water is boiling, slowly add polenta meal while constantly stirring and continue to stir until polenta is thickened (approximately 25 minutes). Stir in the butter and remove from direct heat but keep warm.

Add Porcini and shiitake mushrooms (with half the water from soaking Porcinis), parsley and red bell pepper to the garlic and stir fry for 5 minutes.

Spoon ½ the polenta onto serving platter, then top with a layer of Jack cheese. Cover with remaining ½ polenta. Pour garlic and mushrooms over polenta and serve immediately.

Serves 4.

TOMATO-GARLIC SHORTCAKES

KURT WAIT, Belmont, CA

*C*an you smell the savory, steamy aroma wafting from the fresh, split shortcakes?

SHORTCAKES:

1¼ cups all-purpose flour

1 tablespoon sugar

2 teaspoons baking powder

¼ teaspoon baking soda

¼ teaspoon salt

3 tablespoons butter *or* margarine

3 tablespoons minced fresh garlic

¼ cup plus 2 tablespoons grated Parmesan cheese

½ cup buttermilk

1 egg

TOMATO-GARLIC FILLING:

1 tablespoon minced fresh garlic

3 cups seeded and diced fresh tomato

2 tablespoons finely shredded fresh basil leaves

1 tablespooon balsamic vinegar

1 tablespooon olive oil

Salt

1 cup dairy sour cream *or* plain yogurt

Fresh basil sprigs for garnish, optional

Preheat oven to 400 degrees. In a large bowl, stir together flour, sugar, baking powder, baking soda, and salt. Cut in butter until mixture resembles coarse crumbs. Stir in 2 tablespoons of the garlic and ¼ cup of the Parmesan. In small bowl whisk buttermilk and egg together; add to dry ingredients. Stir until just combined. Transfer dough to lightly floured work surface. Pat into a 6 × 6-inch square. Sprinkle top with remaining 1 tablespoon garlic and 2 tablespoons Parmesan. Cut dough into four equal squares, then cut each square in half diagonally, making 8 triangles. Grease a baking sheet and place shortcakes on it 1 inch apart. Bake for 12 to 15 minutes, or until golden brown.

FILLING & ASSEMBLING:

Combine garlic, tomato, basil, vinegar, and oil. Add salt to taste. Split warm scones and spread with garlic-tomato filling and sour cream. Replace tops and garnish with basil sprigs, if desired.

Makes 8 servings.

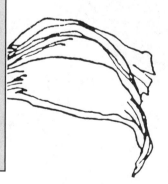

129

*I*t can be gentle, alluring and enticing, giving a marvelous subtle flavor to various dishes —a superb herb.

MARIE RYCKMAN
CINCINNATI ENQUIRER

1994

Gilroy Garlic Festival
July 29, 30, 31, 1994

It's chic to reek!

SIGNATURE MAGAZINE

OIL-FREE ROASTED GARLIC DRESSING

ED GILARDI, Cotati, CA

Oil-free indeed...one would never know. Guaranteed to be one of your favorite recipes.

Place whole heads of garlic in a small baking dish. Bake at 325 degrees until soft, about 1 hour.

When cool enough to handle, separate garlic cloves; squeeze to remove garlic from skins.

Puree garlic, shallot, water, mustard, wine vinegar, and herbs in a food processor or blender until smooth and creamy.

Makes 2 cups.

2	heads fresh garlic
2/3	cup chopped shallot
1/2	cup water
1/4	cup Dijon mustard
3	tablespoons white wine vinegar
2	teaspoons chopped fresh rosemary
2	teaspoons chopped fresh sage

THAI GARLIC SCALLOPS

GEORGE KYSOR, San Leandro, CA

The broiled mango slices not only help in creating a beautiful presentation, but also add to the flavor of these garlic scallops.

2	ripe mangoes
	Black pepper
	Sugar
4	tablespoons unsalted butter, divided
6	large cloves fresh garlic, finely chopped
1	shallot, finely chopped
1	tablespoon curry powder
1	teaspoon flour
1	can (14 oz.) coconut milk (not coconut cream)
1	tablespoon white wine
1/2	tablespoons fresh lemon juice
	Salt
8	oz. sea scallops, rinsed and dried

Peel mangoes; slice. Arrange on a broiler pan. Sprinkle with pepper and sugar; reserve.

To make sauce, sauté garlic and shallot in 2 tablespoons butter until soft, about 2 minutes. Mix curry powder and flour; stir into garlic mixture. Stir in white wine. Reserve a few tablespoons clear liquid from coconut milk; pour remainder into sauce. Bring to a boil; reduce over medium-high heat by half. Add lemon juice; season to taste with salt and pepper. If necessary, thin with reserved coconut liquid. Reserve sauce.

Sauté scallops in remaining 2 tablespoons butter until just firm and opaque, about 3 minutes. Stir scallops into curry sauce. Heat; keep warm.

Broil reserved mango slices until lightly brown, about 2 minutes.

To serve, divide scallops between 2 warmed dinner plates; surround with mango slices.

Makes 2 servings.

131

GRILLED SHRIMP AND ORZO WITH CILANTRO-LIME PESTO

ELAINE MAEDA, North Hollywood, CA

If you like cilantro, then you will love this twist to the pesto sauce.

1/2	cup olive oil
5	large cloves fresh garlic, coarsely chopped
2 1/2	cups loosely packed fresh cilantro
1	cup loosely packed Italian flat leaf parsley
2	tablespoons fresh lime juice
1/2	teaspoon salt
24	large shrimp, shelled and deveined
6	wooden skewers, soaked in water
4	oz. dry orzo (rice shaped pasta)

Heat olive oil in small skillet. Sauté garlic until softened, about 10 minutes. Cool to room temperature.

To make pesto, combine oil and garlic mixture, cilantro, parsley, lime juice, and salt in the work bowl of a food processor. Process until smooth.

Pour enough pesto over shrimp to coat; marinate shrimp in the refrigerator for a few hours.

When ready to serve, cook orzo in salted boiling water until tender, about 3 minutes. Drain; return to pot. Stir in 3/4 cup remaining pesto or to taste; keep warm.

Grill shrimp over medium-hot coals or in the broiler until just firm and opaque, about 3 minutes per side.

Pour orzo on a large, warmed platter; top with skewered shrimp.

Makes 6 servings.

GARLIC PORK KEBOBS

CAROLINE SCHOBER, Vancouver, B.C.

Cashews add a rich, nutty flavor to this quick and easy kebob recipe.

2	tablespoons mayonnaise
1	teaspoon Dijon mustard
5	cloves fresh garlic, finely chopped
1/4	cup finely chopped cashew nuts
1	pork tenderloin, about 1 lb.
4	wooden skewers, soaked in water
	Salt
	Pepper

On a flat plate, mix mayonnaise and mustard. On a second plate mix garlic and nuts. Reserve mixtures.

Cut pork into 1-inch cubes; thread on skewers. Season with salt and pepper.

Dip 1 side of each kebob first in reserved mayonnaise mixture, then in reserved garlic mixture.

Arrange dipped side up on an oiled baking sheet.

Bake at 350 degrees until pork is browned and firm to the touch, about 25 minutes.

Makes 4 servings.

HOT CHICKEN

GINETTE WARK, Temecula, CA

Crushed red pepper heats up this chicken dish.

2	cups thick soy sauce*
1	head (10 to 12 large cloves) fresh garlic, separated and peeled
1½	tablespoons crushed red pepper
	Juice of ½ lemon
3	whole chicken breasts, skin removed
	Black pepper
3½	cups cooked white rice

To make sauce, blend soy sauce, garlic, red pepper and lemon juice in a blender at medium speed; reserve.

Wash chicken in cold water; pat dry. Arrange chicken in a shallow baking dish. Season with pepper. Bake chicken at 350 degrees until firm to the touch, about 25 minutes. Remove from oven; reserve pan with juices. Let chicken cool.

When cool enough to handle, remove chicken from the bone; tear into bite-sized pieces. Return chicken to baking pan. Pour reserved sauce over chicken. Return to 350 degree oven; bake 45 minutes. Baste every 15 minutes. Divide rice and chicken with sauce among 6 warmed plates.

Makes 6 servings.

Note: may be purchased at Asian markets.

TUSCAN WHITE BEAN SOUP

BARBARA MORGAN, Concord, CA

Serve this hearty soup on a cold winter night.

1½	cups chopped onion
2	smoked ham hocks
2	tablespoons unsalted butter
8	cups chicken stock, preferably homemade
1	cup white beans, soaked overnight
4	cloves fresh garlic
¼	teaspoon chopped fresh thyme
1	cup Sonoma dried tomato halves, softened in boiling water; julienned
1	small Nappa cabbage, coarsely chopped
	Salt
	Pepper
	Shaved Parmesan cheese for garnish

In a large soup pot, sauté onions and ham hocks in butter until the onions are golden. Add chicken stock, beans, garlic, and thyme. Bring soup to a boil; reduce to simmer. Simmer until beans are tender, about 1 hour.

Remove ham hocks from soup; dice meat. Return meat to pot; discard bones. Stir in tomato and cabbage. Simmer 15 minutes. Season to taste with salt and pepper. Ladle into 6 warmed soup bowls. Garnish with cheese.

Makes 6 servings.

133

SOUTHWEST BREAD

JIM KELLEY, Washington, DC

This hearty creation would be a delicious accompaniment to soup or salad.

1	package active dry yeast (2 teaspoons)
2	cups warm water
1½	cup honey
¾	cup yogurt
1½	cups yellow cornmeal
1½	cups whole wheat flour
¼	cup chopped fresh garlic
1	cup cooked black beans
½	cup corn, frozen or canned
½	cup chopped red onion
¼	cup chopped fresh cilantro
¼	cup chopped sun-dried tomato, packed in olive oil
3	tablespoons butter, melted
1	tablespoon chili powder
1	teaspoon ground cumin
1	teaspoon salt
½	teaspoon tarragon vinegar
1	mild green chili pepper, seeded; finely chopped
1	jalapeño pepper, seeded; finely chopped
4	cups bread flour
1	egg, beaten

Mix yeast, water, honey, yogurt, cornmeal, and whole wheat flour; reserve mixture until bubbles form, about 1 hour.

Stir in garlic, beans, corn, onion, coriander, tomato, butter, chili powder, cumin, salt, vinegar, chili pepper, and jalapeño pepper. Add flour mixture until a firm dough is achieved. Knead on a lightly floured surface until smooth and elastic, about 5 minutes.

Turn dough in a bowl that has been coated with olive oil. Cover with a tea towel; let rise until double in volume, about 1 hour.

Punch down dough; divide equally into 4 pieces. Form each piece into a ball. Arrange 2 balls of dough seam-side down on each of two oiled baking sheets. Cover with a tea towel; let rise until nearly double in volume, about 1 hour.

Brush dough with egg; slash top of each surface 3 times with a sharp knife or a razor blade. Bake at 375 degrees until golden brown and center reaches 190 degrees, about 25 minutes. Bread should sound hollow when tapped. Cool on wire racks.

Makes 4 loaves.

NANCY & JR'S ROASTED GARLIC RISOTTO

JEANETTE RICE, Campbell, CA

*P*ancetta and roasted garlic enhance the flavor of this creamy risotto.

6	cups beef broth, preferably homemade
1/2	oz. dried porcini mushrooms
3	medium onions, quartered; thinly sliced
2 1/2	tablespoons olive oil
1	cup water
2	oz. thinly sliced pancetta, chopped
1 1/3	cups arborio rice
2	large heads roasted garlic, separated and removed from skins
	Salt
	Pepper
	Asiago cheese, grated, for garnish
2	tablespoons chopped, fresh Italian flat leaf parsley, for garnish

Bring 1 cup broth to a boil; pour over dried mushrooms. Let stand 30 minutes.

Meanwhile, sauté onions in 2 tablespoons of oil in a large skillet over medium-low heat, stirring frequently, until lightly browned, about 20 minutes. Reserve.

Drain mushrooms, reserving liquid. Rinse mushrooms to remove any remaining grit; dice.

Reserve. Strain reserved mushroom liquid through a coffee filter. In a large saucepan, combine mushroom liquid, remaining broth, and water. Bring to a simmer; maintain temperature.

In a large skillet, sauté pancetta in remaining 1/2 teaspoon oil until pancetta is cooked but not browned, about 3 minutes. Stir in rice; cook 2 to 3 minutes, stirring constantly. Over medium heat, add 1 cup reserved hot liquid and mushrooms to rice, stirring constantly. When rice has absorbed liquid, stir in roasted garlic. Continue to add hot liquid, 1/2 cup at a time, stirring constantly, until rice is tender and creamy, about 30 minutes. After 10 minutes, stir in reserved onion. When rice is done, season to taste with salt and pepper. Divide among 6 warmed, flat soup bowls or plates. Garnish with cheese and parsley.

Makes 6 servings.

135

1995

*The Gilroy Garlic Festival
is a mentionable part of
the California experience.*
SAN FRANCISCO EXAMINER

GARLIC-LACED SHRIMP CAKES WITH CORN & AVOCADO SALSA

KURT WAIT, Redwood City, CA

Kurt presents this colorful dish on a red plate, garnished with fresh lemon slices and a bright yellow carnation. Place the salsa in a white bowl in the center, surrounded by the shrimp cakes.

SALSA:
- 1 cup cooked corn kernels
- 1 cup diced plum tomato
- 1 avocado, pitted, peeled, and diced
- 1 tablespoon chopped fresh thyme
- 1 tablespoon finely chopped fresh garlic
- 1 tablespoon lemon juice
- 1 tablespoon olive oil
- 1/4 teaspoon salt
- 1/8 teaspoon cayenne pepper

SHRIMP CAKES:
- 40 cloves fresh garlic, unpeeled
- 12 oz. cooked shrimp, coarsely chopped
- 1/4 cup light sour cream or plain yogurt
- 2/3 cup dry bread crumbs, divided
- 2 eggs
- 2 tablespoons olive oil
- 1 tablespoon chopped fresh thyme
- 1 tablespoon finely chopped fresh garlic

SALSA:
Gently fold all ingredients together. Refrigerate.

SHRIMP CAKES:
Roast garlic at 350 degrees in a greased 1 quart baking dish covered with foil until tender, about 30 minutes. Cool. Squeeze garlic into bowl; mash. Stir in shrimp, 1/3 cup bread crumbs, sour cream, eggs, and thyme until well blended. Shape shrimp mixture into 8 one-inch thick patties. Mix remaining bread crumbs with chopped garlic; coat patties with bread crumb mixture. Heat oil in a non-stick skillet over medium heat. Brown patties until crisp, turning over once, about 5 minutes on each side. Serve with salsa.

GILROY GARLIC VAMPIRE SOUP

PETER ANELLO, Morgan Hill, CA

*Peter's chicken stock-based soup melds onions and garlic
in a subtle blend of herbs and cream.*

2	tablespoons olive oil
2	yellow onions, thinly sliced
	Pinch of sugar
10	cloves fresh garlic, smashed and peeled
1	tablespoon garlic, chopped
2	bay leaves
1/2	teaspoon salt
1/8	teaspoon freshly ground black pepper
2	quarts reduced salt chicken broth
1	teaspoon pesto, or chopped fresh basil leaves
1	teaspoon chopped fresh thyme
2	cups firmly packed, diced, day-old French bread
	Dash hot pepper sauce, or to taste
	Dash Worcestershire sauce, or to taste
1/2	cup whipping cream
1/3	cup freshly grated Parmesan cheese

Heat oil in a large stock pot; stir in onion and sugar. Sauté until onion just begins to brown, about 5 minutes. Stir in smashed garlic cloves, bay leaves, salt, and pepper; sauté until onion is a rich, golden brown, about 5 minutes. Stir in broth, chopped garlic, pesto, and thyme. Bring to a boil.

Reduce heat to low; simmer until vegetables are very soft, about 35 minutes. Remove bay leaves.

Stir in bread; simmer, stirring constantly, until bread falls apart and thickens soup, about 10 minutes. Stir in hot pepper sauce and Worcestershire sauce. Remove from heat; puree with an electric hand blender or in batches in a conventional blender or food processor. Heat, but do not boil, stirring in cream and cheese.

Makes 4 to 6 servings.

138

CARAMELIZED GARLIC CROSTINI

ROXANNE CHAN, Albany CA

Be sure not to miss a step in the carmalizing process.

2	tablespoons olive oil
1	cup fresh garlic cloves, peeled and slivered
4	large cloves fresh garlic, finely chopped
1	cup dry white wine, divided
1/4	cup Balsamic vinegar
1	tablespoon sugar
2	oz. soft, fresh goat cheese
1	tablespoon chopped fresh mint leaves
1/2	teaspoon coarsely ground black pepper
8	diagonal slices of Italian or French bread, about 1/2 inch thick
	Mint sprigs (optional)
	Carrot curls (optional)

Heat 1 tablespoon oil in skillet over medium heat. Stir in slivered garlic, 1/2 cup white wine, vinegar, and sugar. Bring to a boil; continue boiling, stirring frequently, until almost all liquid evaporates, about 10 minutes. Stir in 1/2 cup white wine, boil until liquid evaporate. Stir in remaining 1/2 cup white wine; simmer until mixture is syrupy. Keep garlic mixture warm.

Toast bread on each side; brush one side of each with remaining 1 tablespoon olive oil; reserve.

Mix together cheese, chopped garlic, mint, and pepper. Spread cheese mixture on oiled side of toast. Top each toast with garlic mixture. Garnish with mint and carrot.

Makes 8 servings.

TERIYAKI GARLIC

DONALD DEZAN, San Diego, CA

Dezan, a former U.S. Marine, was inspired to make this teriyaki garlic after tasting it in Korea in 1977.

30	to 40 heads fresh garlic
1	cup lite soy sauce
1	cup sake
1	cup packed brown sugar
1/2	cup rice wine vinegar
1	thumb-sized piece ginger, peeled

Gently break garlic heads apart; discard any cloves that are not firm and smooth. Do not peel.

Select a large, wide-mouth jar that will hold the garlic.

Bring remaining ingredients to a simmer, stirring frequently. Stir in garlic cloves; boil 1 minute.

Remove from heat. Cover; let stand until cool. Gently stir with a wooden spoon to loosen skins slightly. Ladle into the jar; pour sauce over to cover. If short of sauce, add additional soy, sake, and rice wine vinegar, keeping proportions the same. Cover tightly; let rest at room temperature for 24 hours. Shake jar to remove air bubbles.

Refrigerate; marinate for several weeks. Sample a clove after 2 weeks. If garlic is too crisp, drain sauce; bring to a boil. Pour over garlic; cool. Return to refrigerator. Garlic will keep 6 to 8 months in the refrigerator.

Serve as a condiment with beer, sausage, and cheese.

Makes 1 jar.

139

THE GREAT WHITE PIZZA

SANDRA SCHINNEER, Springfield, IL

Pizza without a red sauce? It can be done, and this will become a favorite real quick.

DOUGH:

1	package dry yeast
1	cup tepid water
2	tablespoons extra-virgin olive oil
2¾	cups bread or all-purpose flour

TOPPINGS:

2	tablespoons extra-virgin olive oil
1	head fresh garlic, peeled and finely chopped
2	cups shredded Mozzarella cheese
1	red bell pepper, stem, seeds, and membranes removed, sliced into thin rings
1	cup sliced fresh mushrooms
¼	cup sliced ripe olives
¼	cup freshly grated Parmesan or Romano cheese
½	cup crumbled Roquefort or Blue cheese
1½	tablespoons crushed dried basil leaves

In large mixing bowl, stir yeast into water. Let yeast dissolve, about 5 minutes. Stir in olive oil.

Stir in half the flour; beat with a wooden spoon until gluten develops. Mix in remaining flour; turn onto a floured board. Knead dough until smooth and elastic, about 5 minutes. Return to bowl; brush with a little olive oil. Let rise until doubled in volume, about 1 hour. Punch dough down; divide in half. Reserve half for another pizza (dough freezes well).

Spray a 14 to 16-inch pizza pan with non-stick spray. Stretch dough to edges of pan. Spread olive oil over dough. Scatter garlic over oil. Layer remaining ingredients in order listed. Bake at 475 degrees until cheese browns lightly and crust is crisp, about 10 minutes. Cut in 8 slices.

Makes 8 slices.

140

SPICY GARLIC CHILI

KELLI LARKSPUR-HONDA, Gilroy, CA

*K*elli had been making this chili for years but revised the recipe especially
for the garlic festival—making it with 60 cloves of garlic.

6	lbs. boneless pork butt, cut in 1-inch cubes
2	yellow onions, chopped
60	cloves fresh garlic, chopped or 1 cup chopped garlic from a jar
1/2	cup finely chopped fresh jalapeño peppers (with seeds)
1	tablespoon packed dark brown sugar
1	can (28 oz.) crushed tomatoes with juice
1/4	cup molasses
2	oz. unsweetened chocolate, melted
3/4	cup chili powder
1/4	cup ground cumin
1	tablespoon dried basil leaves
1	tablespoon plus 2 teaspoons dried oregano
2	teaspoons dry mustard
1	teaspoon dried coriander
1	teaspoon freshly ground black pepper
1/2	teaspoon ground cloves
24	oz. dark beer
3	cups boiling water
1/4	cup dry red wine or cider vinegar
3	tablespoons soy sauce
1	tablespoon plus 2 teaspoons salt
1/4	cup purchased habanero pepper sauce (very hot) or to taste
	Sour cream for garnish
	Chopped, fresh cilantro for garnish

Day before serving, in a Dutch oven over high heat,
brown pork until crispy and as much fat as possible has
been rendered. Remove pork with a slotted spoon; drain
well in a colander lined with paper towel. Leave 1/4 cup
drippings in the Dutch oven; refrigerate remainder. Over
medium-low heat, stir in onion, garlic, and jalapeño;
sauté until vegetables are soft, about 10 minutes. Stir in
brown sugar; cook a few minutes more. Remove from
heat. Stir in tomato, molasses, and melted chocolate; stir
in spices and reserved pork. Refrigerate overnight.

Heat refrigerated chili mixture. Remove solidified fat
from reserved drippings; discard. Stir remaining juices
into chili. Stir in beer, boiling water, red wine or vinegar,
soy sauce, and salt.

Bring to a boil, stirring frequently. Reduce heat, cover,
simmer, stirring occasionally, until meat is very tender
and flavors have married, about 1 1/2 hours. Stir in
habanero sauce to taste; simmer, covered, for 1/2 hour.
Garnish each serving with sour cream and cilantro.

Makes 8 to 10 servings.

1996

GILROY GARLIC FESTIVAL JULY 26, 27, 28, 1996

142

Today, garlic has been accepted as a necessary part of the total culinary experience and I say "Hooray!"
SAN JOSE MERCURY NEWS

GARLIC COUNTRY CORNMEAL SCONES

PATRICIA LEE HENRY, Moreno Valley, CA

Include these delightful cornmeal treats in your next Sunday brunch, or serve with soup or salad.

GARLIC MIXTURE:
- 1/4 cup chopped fresh elephant garlic or, for a stronger flavor, regular fresh garlic
- 1/3 cup butter or margarine
- 2 tablespoons chopped fresh cilantro
- 1 to 2 drops hot pepper sauce

TOPPING:
- 2 tablespoons all-purpose flour
- 2 teaspoons cornmeal
- 1/2 teaspoon sugar

DOUGH:
- 1 cup yellow cornmeal plus 1 teaspoon
- 1 2/3 cups all-purpose flour
- 4 teaspoons baking powder
- 5 teaspoons sugar
- 1/2 teaspoon salt
- 1 egg, beaten
- 1/2 to 3/4 cup buttermilk

GARLIC MIXTURE:

Sauté garlic in butter until tender, about 3 minutes; stir in cilantro and hot pepper sauce. Cool.

TOPPING:

Combine flour, cornmeal, sugar, and 1 tablespoon garlic mixture; reserve.

DOUGH:

Sprinkle buttered baking sheet with 1 teaspoon cornmeal; reserve. Mix remaining 1 cup cornmeal, flour, baking powder, sugar, and salt. Stir in remaining garlic mixture, egg, and enough buttermilk to form a moist dough. Lightly knead dough on a floured surface 5 or 6 times. Divide dough in half; shape each half into a ball; pat each ball into a 6 inch round. Lightly press half of reserved topping into each round. Cut each round all the way through into 6 wedges but do not separate.

Arrange on prepared baking sheet. Bake at 400 degrees until golden brown, about 20 minutes. Serve warm.

Makes 6 scones.

143

TAILS OF SHRIMP & THE GREAT GARLIC CAPER

RONI GEHLKE, Antioch, CA

Roni has fun using lots of zesty herbs in this shrimp dish.

1	lb. large shrimp, deveined and butterflied
2	tablespoons all-purpose flour
1/2	cup dry white wine
2	tablespoons fresh lemon juice
1	tablespoon capers
1/4	teaspoon *each* dried basil, marjoram, oregano, crushed bay leaf, and rosemary*
1/8	teaspoon freshly ground black pepper
1/2	teaspoon hot pepper sauce, or to taste (optional)
1	tablespoon butter or margarine
6	cloves fresh garlic, finely chopped
1/4	cup sliced mushrooms
2	cups hot, cooked white rice

Toss shrimp with flour; reserve. To make sauce, stir together wine, lemon juice, capers, herbs, pepper and hot sauce; reserve.

Melt butter in wok or large frying pan; over medium-high heat, stir-fry garlic for about 15 seconds. Stir in reserved shrimp and mushrooms; stir-fry until shrimp is just firm and opaque, about 3 minutes. Remove shrimp; reserve.

Stir reserved sauce into hot pan. Cook over high heat until sauce boils. Stir reserved shrimp mixture into sauce; serve immediately over rice.

Makes 4 servings.

1 1/4 teaspoons dried Italian Seasonings may be substituted.

GARLIC & SMOKED OYSTER SPREAD

WANDA ANN HAMMILL, Kennewick, WA

Toasting the walnuts first enhances the flavor of this oyster spread.

144

1/2	cup fresh garlic cloves
3	cups smoked Brady's oysters
2	tablespoons chopped onion
3	tablespoons lemon juice
1	cup Blue cheese, crumbled
2	packages (8 oz. each) cream cheese, at room temperature
1/2	cup butter
2	cups toasted walnuts, finely chopped

In food processor, finely chop garlic, oysters, and onion with lemon juice. Add cheeses and butter, process until smooth. Refrigerate mixture until firm but not hard. Shape into a ball or log; roll in chopped nuts, lightly pressing nuts into cheese. Refrigerate, tightly wrapped. Serve with toasted sourdough rounds.

Makes approximately 1 1/2 quarts.

ROASTED GARLIC AND PEPPERS WITH POLENTA POINTS

MADONNA FINNEY ELLIOT, Tallahassee, FL

Another creative way to serve polenta.

2	heads fresh garlic
2	cups chicken broth, divided
3	tablespoons olive oil divided
2	red bell peppers, cut in strips
1	tablespoon chopped fresh basil
	Salt
	Freshly ground black pepper
1	cup water
2/3	cup polenta (coarse corn meal)
1/4	cup grated Parmesan cheese

Roast garlic by removing papery outer skin, leaving heads intact; arrange whole heads in a small baking dish. Pour 1/2 cup broth in the bottom of the pan; drizzle garlic with 2 tablespoons olive oil.

Bake at 350 degrees, covered, until garlic is soft, about 1 1/4 hours. When cool enough to handle, separate cloves. Squeeze cloves out of skin; reserve.

Roast bell peppers by arranging skin side up on an oiled baking dish; bake at 425 degrees until skins are blistered, about 20 minutes. Immediately put in a paper bag; close tightly. Let pepper strips rest in the bag until cool; remove skin.

Pour remaining 1 tablespoon olive oil over pepper strips combined with reserved garlic; sprinkle with basil. Lightly season with salt and pepper; reserve.

Make polenta by bringing water and remaining 1 1/2 cups broth to a boil. Stirring constantly, drizzle polenta into the boiling water; reduce heat to very low. Cook, stirring occasionally, until polenta thickens and pulls away from the side of the pan, and tastes "cooked," about 20 minutes.

Stir in cheese. Pour and spread evenly into a buttered 9 x 13-inch pan; refrigerate, covered, until firm, about 2 hours. Turn polenta onto a cutting board; cut into 12 squares. Cut each square into 2 triangles; arrange on a lightly oiled baking sheet. Bake at 325 degrees turning once, until polenta is browned on both sides, about 25 minutes.

Assemble dish by arranging pepper strips and roasted garlic over polenta. Serve warm or at room temperature.

Makes 6 servings.

145

ROASTED GARLIC CHEESECAKE WITH WARM TOMATO SAUCE

JUDY SAMUEL-KEYES, Gilroy, CA

Judy says not to be fooled by the name of this dish. "It isn't a sweet pie," she said. "You can probably eat it with a cold salad or roasted chicken."

ROASTED GARLIC:

2	heads fresh garlic
2	teaspoons olive oil
	Salt

CRUST:

3	cups water
1/2	teaspoon salt
1	cup polenta (coarse cornmeal)
1	tablespoon butter
1/2	teaspoon dried thyme or oregano

FILLING:

3	cups chopped, sweet onion (such as Maui or Vidallia)
3	tablespoons butter
2	8 oz. packages cream cheese, at room temperature
1	cup ricotta cheese
1	teaspoon salt
1/4	teaspoon cayenne pepper
5	eggs

WARM TOMATO SAUCE:

1	cup chopped onion
3	tablespoons olive oil
2	cans (28 oz.) crushed tomatoes with puree*
1	teaspoon onion powder
1/2	to 1 teaspoon garlic powder
	Jalapeño peppers, seeded; finely chopped
	Salt
	Pepper

ROASTED GARLIC:

Remove papery outer skin, leaving heads intact; arrange whole heads in a small baking dish.

Drizzle garlic with olive oil; sprinkle with salt. Bake at 350 degrees, covered, until garlic is soft, about 1 1/4 hours. When cool enough to handle, separate cloves. Squeeze cloves out of skin; reserve.

CRUST:

Bring water to a boil; stir in salt. Stirring constantly, drizzle polenta into the boiling water. Reduce heat to very low; stir in butter and herb. Cook, stirring occasionally, until polenta thickens and pulls away from the side of the pan, and tastes "cooked," about 20 minutes. Pour polenta into an oiled, 10-inch spring form pan; spread evenly over bottom with a spoon. (Frequently dipping spoon in cold water will make it easier.) Reserve.

FILLING:

In a non-stick frying pan, cook onion in butter over very low heat, stirring frequently, until golden brown, about 25 minutes; cool. Reserve. With an electric mixer (do not use a food processor or blender), beat together cream cheese, ricotta, salt, and cayenne. Beat in cool reserved garlic. Beat in cooled reserved onion; beat in eggs 1 at a time. Pour mixture into prepared pan. Bake at 350 degrees for 1 hour. Turn oven off; leave cheesecake in the oven for 15 minutes. Remove from oven; let cool about 1 hour. Serve sliced with Warm Tomato Sauce.

WARM TOMATO SAUCE:

Sauté onion in olive oil until translucent, about 5 minutes. Stir in tomato and onion and garlic powder. Season to taste with salt and pepper. Simmer until flavors marry, about 1 hour. Mexican-style variation: Make cheesecake crust with oregano. To the sauce, add a few finely chopped jalapeño peppers with the onion along with 1 teaspoon cumin. When sauce is done, stir in 1/4 cup chopped fresh cilantro.

In the summer, an equal amount of fresh, peeled, seeded, and diced very ripe tomatoes may be substituted.

146

ROASTED GARLIC POTATO SALAD

MARGARET BAVARO, Colts Neck, NJ

Roasted garlic and sun-dried tomatoes dress up this warm potato salad.

- 1/4 cup Balsamic vinegar
- 1/2 teaspoon salt
- 1/4 teaspoon freshly ground black pepper
- 3/4 cup olive oil, divided
- 1 head fresh garlic
- 2 lbs. new potatoes, halved if small, quartered if medium
- 4 green onions, thinly sliced
- 1/2 cup whole oil-cured black olives, then pit and slice
- 1/4 cup oil-cured sun-dried tomatoes, cut in thin strips

To make dressing, mix vinegar, salt, and pepper; beat in 1/2 cup oil. Reserve.

To roast garlic, remove papery outer skin, leaving head intact; put in a small baking dish. Drizzle garlic with 1 tablespoon olive oil. Bake a 450 degrees, covered, until garlic is soft, about 45 minutes. When cool enough to handle, separate cloves. Squeeze cloves out of skin; reserve.

While garlic bakes, toss onion and potato in 3 table-spoons olive oil in a 9 x 12-inch baking dish.

Bake uncovered along side garlic, stirring every 10 minutes, until potatoes are tender and lightly browned, about 30 minutes.

Gently toss hot potato mixture with olives, tomato, reserved garlic, and reserved dressing. Serve at room temperature.

Makes 8 servings.

ITALIAN SAUSAGE & GARLIC SOUP

EVERINE E. WEIMER, Anaheim, CA

This couldn't be easier to prepare—or heartier to consume.

- 8 oz. sweet Italian sausage, bulk or links
- 1 medium onion, chopped
- 2 cans (14 1/2 oz. each) chicken broth
- 2 medium potatoes, peeled and diced
- 1 large, red bell pepper, julienned
- 6 cloves fresh garlic, finely chopped
- 1 bunch spinach, chopped
- 1/2 lb. mushrooms, sliced
- 1 cup beer
- 1 teaspoon crushed red pepper
- 1 teaspoon coarsely ground black pepper

For sausage links, remove casing. Sauté sausage and onion, stirring to break up sausage, until sausage is browned, about 5 minutes. Stir in remaining ingredients; bring to boil. Reduce heat; simmer, covered, until potatoes are tender, about 20 minutes.

Makes 4 servings.

147

1997

*G*arlic: *comin' on strong!*

THE TORONTO SUN

ROASTED GARLIC AND OLIVE PEPPERCORN SPREAD

LINDA FAYE WYLIE, Phoenix, AZ

Peppercorns add zip to this roasted garlic and olive spread.

15	cloves fresh garlic, peeled
1	tablespoon peppercorns
1/4	cup olive oil
1/2	cup Calamati olives, pitted
1/2	cup green olives, pitted

Roast garlic and peppercorns in oil in a covered pan at 350 degrees until garlic is tender, about 30 minutes. Drain excess oil from garlic. Puree garlic and peppercorns; add olives. Puree until smooth. Refrigerate overnight to marry flavors.

Makes approximately 1 cup.

SIZZLING GARLIC & CITRUS SHRIMP

ELLEN BURR, Truro, MA

The citrus juices add a wonderful flavor to this shrimp recipe.

24	jumbo shrimp, about 1 1/2 lbs, peeled (tails on) and deveined
1/3	cup fresh lime juice
1/3	cup fresh lemon juice
1/3	cup blood orange juice
4	oz. unsalted butter, melted
12	large cloves fresh garlic, peeled and finely chopped
	Salt to taste
1/4	cup chopped, fresh cilantro
1/4	teaspoon Pico de Gallo or cayenne pepper
1	large loaf French bread, thinly sliced
	Citrus slices for garnish
	Cilantro leaves for garnish

Arrange shrimp in a large, shallow non-reactive baking dish. To make sauce, mix remaining ingredients except bread; pour over shrimp. Cook shrimp and sauce under the broiler, turning shrimp once or twice, until shrimp is opaque and just firm to the touch, about 8 minutes.

Immediately serve shrimp and sauce over thin slices of French bread. Garnish with citrus slices and sprigs of cilantro. Serve remaining bread on the side.

Variation: Substitute 1 1/2 pounds scallops or calamari rings for shrimp; adjust cooking time as needed.

149

MARINATED GARLIC AND PEPPER FRESH CHEESE

KAREN DAVIS, Oklahoma City, OK

This tasty appetizer can be made early in the day.

1 lb. fresh, white cheese, such as goat cheese, cream cheese or Mexican cheese

2 cups fresh garlic cloves (approximately 5 to 6 heads)

1/3 cup Szechwan peppercorns (mixed whole peppercorns may be substituted)

8 oz. extra-virgin olive oil

1 tablespoon Vietnamese chili-garlic sauce or to taste (hot pepper sauce may be substituted)

Freshly chopped cilantro, basil or mint for garnish

Toasted pumpkin seed kernels or pine nuts for garnish

Thinly sliced toasted French bread or crackers

Slice cheese about 1/3 inch thick; arrange in a single layer in an ovenproof glass baking dish.

Refrigerate. Blanch garlic in boiling water for 10 minutes; cool to room temperature. Drain. Peel; reserve.

Roast peppercorns in a heavy pan over high heat, shaking frequently. As soon as the peppercorns become aromatic, reduce heat; stir in reserved garlic and oil. Cook over low heat, stirring frequently, until garlic is soft, about 10 minutes. Stir in the chili-garlic sauce; pour mixture over reserved cheese. Marinate at room temperature for 4 hours or in refrigerator at least 8 hours. Bring to room temperature before serving. Garnish and serve with bread or crackers.

GILROY-STYLE STUFFED GRAPE LEAVES GREMOLATA

ROXANNE E. CHAN, Albany, CA

If you have never tried stuffed grape leaves, don't pass up this recipe.
It's a real palate pleaser.

GRAPE LEAVES:

1	cup finely chopped fresh garlic
1/4	lb. portabello mushrooms, coarsely chopped
2	tablespoons olive oil, divided
1/3	cup coarsely chopped toasted hazelnuts
1	jar grape leaves, rinsed and drained
1/2	cup crumbled fresh goat cheese

DRESSING:

2	tablespoons olive oil
1	tablespoon lemon juice
1/2	teaspoon grated lemon zest
1/4	teaspoon lemon-pepper seasoning
1	tablespoon chopped, fresh parsley
1	tablespoon thinly sliced chives
4	cloves fresh garlic, finely chopped

GARNISH:

Chives and parsley leaves
Lemon slices

GRAPE LEAVES:

Sauté garlic and mushroom in 1 tablespoon olive oil until vegetables are tender and any liquid has evaporated, about 5 minutes. Stir in nuts; cool. Put a grape leaf shiny-side down with stem end toward you. Put 1 tablespoon garlic mixture about 1/2 inch from the bottom edge of the leaf; sprinkle a little goat cheese on top of filling. Fold in the sides of the leaf, overlapping slightly; roll up. Repeat until all filling is used. (Use remaining leaves to line a serving plate.) Brush stuffed grape leaves with remaining 1 tablespoon oil. Broil, turning once, until grape leaves are hot, about 3 minutes per side. Arrange on leaf-lined serving platter.

DRESSING:

Mix oil with remaining ingredients; drizzle over stuffed grape leaves. Garnish with chives, parsley leaves, and lemon slices.

Makes approximately 1 1/2 dozen.

151

GRILLED SALMON TROUT FILLETS WITH ROASTED GARLIC SALSA

BARBARA J. MORGAN, Concord, CA

Barbara shares another wonderful fish recipe. Be sure to refrigerate the salsa once it has been prepared so that the flavors are well blended.

SALSA:

6	heads fresh garlic, roasted
1/4	cup olive oil
1/3	cup finely diced red onion
1/3	cup finely diced red bell pepper
1/3	cup chopped fresh cilantro
1	can (4 oz.) diced green chiles
2	tablespoons seasoned rice wine vinegar
1	tablespoon sherry vinegar
1	teaspoon fresh lemon juice
1	teaspoon honey

TROUT:

1/3	cup olive oil
2	teaspoons grated lemon zest
2	tablespoons finely chopped garlic
1/2	teaspoon salt
1/4	teaspoon freshly ground black pepper
6	salmon trout fillets (approximately 6 oz. each)

SALSA:

Cut off the top 1/4 inch of each garlic head. Drizzle olive oil over garlic heads and season with salt and pepper. Wrap each head completely in aluminum foil and place in preheated 350-degree oven for 25 to 30 minutes or until garlic is very soft when squeezed. Remove from oven and allow to cool.

Squeeze garlic from each clove; mix with remaining ingredients. Refrigerate to marry flavors.

TROUT:

Whisk together olive oil, and next 4 ingredients. Rub mixture over trout; marinate for 1 hour. Grill trout over medium-hot charcoal until trout is just firm to the touch, about 3 minutes on each side.

Divide trout among 6 plates; top each with a heaping tablespoon of salsa.

Makes 6 servings.

152

CORNMEAL GARLIC PANCAKES WITH MANGO SYRUP

KIM LANDHUIS, Fort Dodge, IA

A special treat for two on a special occasion. The mango syrup brightens up these little garlic cornmeal pancakes.

SYRUP:
1 1/2 cups diced, ripe mango
1/3 cup sugar
1/2 cup strawberry jelly
1 tablespoon lemon juice

PANCAKES:
1/4 cup chopped fresh garlic
1/4 cup canola oil, divided
1/2 cup skim milk
1 egg, beaten
1/2 cup flour
1/2 cup cornmeal
1 tablespoon sugar
2 teaspoons baking powder

SYRUP:

Combine all ingredients; bring to a boil over medium heat. Reduce to simmer; continue simmering until sugar dissolves. Reserve.

PANCAKES:

Sauté garlic in 2 tablespoons oil over medium heat until golden. Drain garlic on paper towel.

Whisk together garlic with remaining ingredients until smooth. Heat the same skillet over medium heat; pour 1/4 cup batter into pan. When bubbles begin to break, turn to the other side; cook until golden, about 1 minute. Repeat until all batter is gone, using remaining oil as needed. Keep cooked pancakes warm in the oven.

Serve pancakes with warm mango syrup.

Makes 2 servings.

TIPSY BRISKET

SUE VOGELSANGER, Rocklin, CA

Tipsy...yet wide awake!

4 to 5 lbs. beef brisket
15 to 20 cloves garlic, peeled
1 medium white onion, coarsely chopped
1 cup white wine
1/2 cup bourbon
1/2 cup water
1/4 cup strong brewed coffee
2 teaspoons freshly ground black pepper
1/2 teaspoon salt

Put brisket fat side up in a 9 1/2 x 13 1/2 x 2-inch ovenproof glass baking dish. Roast uncovered at 350 degrees for 1 hour. Remove from oven; pour wine, bourbon, water, and coffee over brisket.

Sprinkle garlic and onion in juice around meat. Cover with foil, bake at 325 degrees until meat is very tender, about 2 hours. Remove from oven; cool. Refrigerate overnight.

To serve, remove meat to a cutting board; reserve liquid; slice thinly across grain. Reserve.

Skim fat from liquid. Arrange reserved meat slices in liquid; baste. Sprinkle with pepper and salt.

Cover; heat at 300 degrees until dish is hot and bubbly, about 45 minutes.

Makes 8 to 10 servings.

153

1998

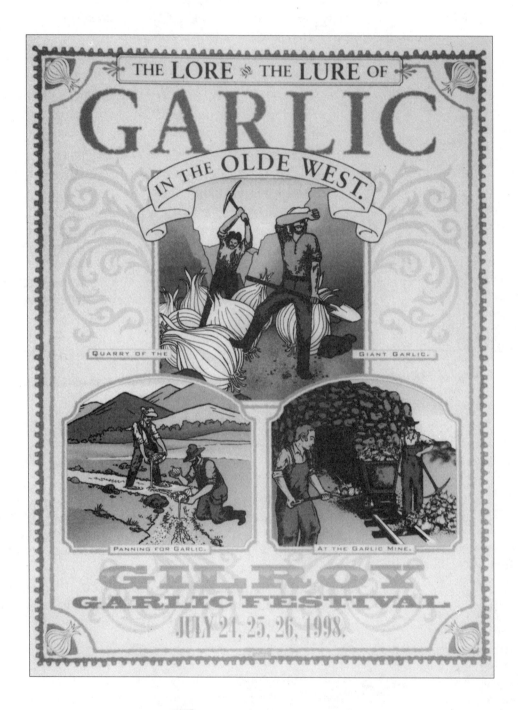

*It was rollicking good fun
and the food was super.*
SAN FRANCISCO CHRONICLE

FLAMBOYANT FLANK STEAK WITH FRAGRANT FILLING

FRANCES BENTHIN, Scio, OR

Flank your flank steak with roasted baby potatoes and steamed baby carrots for a cozy winter supper.

MARINADE:

6	cloves fresh garlic
1/4	cup hoisin sauce
1/4	cup dry red wine
2	tablespoons honey
2	tablespoons Asian (toasted) sesame oil
1	tablespoon chopped fresh rosemary

FLANK STEAK:

1	1 1/2 lb., approximately, flank steak
2	heads roasted garlic*
1/2	cup dry bread crumbs
1/4	cup roasted red bell pepper, finely chopped
1/4	cup mascarpone cheese
2	tablespoons Dijon mustard
1/2	teaspoon seasoned salt
1/4	teaspoon cayenne pepper

GARNISH:

Chopped, fresh garlic, as needed
Rosemary sprigs, as needed
Red bell pepper strips, as needed

MARINADE:

Put garlic and remaining ingredients in a blender; process until smooth. Reserve. Lightly score flank steak in a diamond pattern on both sides. In a heavy duty plastic bag with seal, pour reserved marinade over flank steak; seal. Marinate in the refrigerator at least 1 hour, turning occasionally.

FILLING:

Squeeze garlic from cloves; mix with remaining ingredients. Reserve. Just before cooking, remove flank steak from marinade; pat dry. Spread reserved garlic mixture over steak. Starting at the long edge, tightly roll steak in jelly-roll fashion. Cut into 6 equal pieces; secure each with a skewer.

Cook over medium-hot charcoal or in the broiler until steak is just firm to the touch, about 3 to 4 minutes per side.

Garnish each serving with garlic, rosemary, and bell pepper strips.

Makes 6 servings.

To roast garlic, cut 1/4 inch off top of garlic heads. Drizzle with olive oil; lightly sprinkle with salt and pepper. Wrap in foil; bake at 350 degrees until soft, about 30 minutes.

155

VAMPIRE KILLER CHEESECAKE

JOHN and LINDA HIGGINS, San Jose, CA

This is so rich and tasty—even vampires can't resist it.

6	tablespoons butter, divided
1⅓	cups garlic-herb bread crumbs
8	oz. fresh mushrooms, finely chopped
1	cup green onion, thinly sliced
2	tablespoons flour
3	packages (8 oz. each) cream cheese
1	15 oz. container ricotta cheese
½	cup milk
3	eggs
	Freshly ground pepper
3/4	cup fresh garlic, finely chopped
½	cup dried tomato, drained oil-packed or dehydrated reconstituted in boiling water, chopped
½	cup (or more to taste) prepared pesto
½	cup (or more to taste) black olives, finely chopped

Melt 4 tablespoons butter; combine with bread crumbs. Press mixture into the bottom of a 12-inch springform pan sprayed with non-stick spray; reserve.

Sauté mushroom and green onion in remaining 2 tablespoons butter until vegetables are soft, about 3 minutes; sprinkle with flour. Stirring constantly, cook until ingredients are well incorporated, about 1 minute; reserve. In a large bowl, beat cream cheese, ricotta, and milk until smooth. Beat in eggs one at a time. Stir in pepper to taste; stir in garlic and mushroom mixture until thoroughly incorporated. Pour into prepared crust; put pan in a 350-degree oven. Set a pan of hot water on the rack below the cheesecake. Bake cheesecake until center is set, about 60 minutes. Run knife around edge of cake; cool. Refrigerate.

To serve, remove pan sides; set cheesecake on a serving platter. Sprinkle tomato in a circle in the center. Surround with a ring of pesto; finish with a ring of olives. Cut cheesecake into thin wedges. Serve with crackers or sourdough French bread.

Makes 6 servings.

156

GARLIC CHICKEN A L'ORANGE

AILEENE EDSINGER, Morgan Hill, CA

The sweetness of the orange makes an exquisite contrast to the savory garlic.

2	chickens, about 3 lb. each
3	oranges, separated
12	cloves fresh garlic, quartered
1	piece ginger root (about 4 inches), peeled and cut into 4 chunks
	Salt
	Pepper
1	14½ oz. can chicken broth
1	tablespoon cornstarch
3	cups hot, cooked rice
	Orange slices for garnish

Remove innards from chicken; discard or reserve for other use. Thoroughly rinse chickens; pat dry. Reserve.

Quarter 2 oranges. Put 4 orange wedges, half the chopped garlic, and half the ginger in each cavity. Season chickens with salt and pepper. Put chickens breast-side up in a shallow roasting pan. Roast at 350 degrees for 1 hour, basting every 20 minutes with pan juices.

Remove chickens from oven; strain pan juices into a sauce pan; reserve. Remove contents of each cavity over sauce pan into a sieve, pressing solids to release liquid. Discard orange and ginger, reserving garlic. Return chickens to oven; continue to roast until juices run yellow and drumstick wiggles easily, about 15 minutes.

To make sauce, heat cooking juices, add juice from remaining orange and all but ½ cup chicken broth. While liquid heats, mash garlic. Whisk together garlic, ½ cup reserved chicken broth, and cornstarch; whisk mixture into simmering cooking juices. Simmer until thickened, about 2 minutes.

When chicken is done, let rest covered with a tea towel for 10 minutes. Cut into serving-sized pieces. Arrange chicken and rice on a serving platter; drizzle with sauce. Garnish with orange slices.

Makes 6 servings.

For a spicy flavor, add ½ teaspoon crushed red pepper to sauce.

157

GAZPACHO AJO BLANCO

(White Gazpacho with Grapes and Garlic Chips)

SUSAN ASANOVIC, Wilton, CT

This is a rich, flavorful soup that makes a delightful starter to a Mediterranean-style supper, or stands on its own as a lovely light lunch.

2	small heads fresh garlic, separated into cloves, unpeeled
1	seedless English cucumber, peeled and cut into 1-inch chunks
3/4	cup plus 2 tablespoons sliced, blanched almonds, lightly toasted, divided
1 1/4	cups seedless green grapes plus 16 for garnish (do not substitute red grapes)
3	slices day-old rustic bread, crusts removed and torn into bits
2	cups ice cubes
6	oz. brut sparkling wine or Champagne (sparkling water may be substituted)
	Iced water, as needed
	Olive oil as needed for frying
2	tablespoons torn, fresh mint
1	tablespoon torn, fresh tarragon

Blanch garlic in boiling water for 2 minutes. Plunge into cold water; peel. Reserve half for garnish. Finely dice enough cucumber to make 1/4 cup; reserve for garnish. In a blender, puree remaining garlic, remaining cucumber, and 3/4 cup almonds. Add 1 1/4 cups grapes; puree. Reserve in blender. Immerse bread in cold water; squeeze out excess water. Add bread, 1 cup ice cubes, and wine to blender; puree. Add remaining ice cubes; puree until smooth. Strain, pressing to extract liquid. Thin with ice water, as needed, to achieve the consistency of light cream; chill.

To make garnish, slice lengthwise 8 of the largest remaining cloves of garlic (reserve remaining cloves for another use). Sauté garlic slices in 1/4 inch hot olive oil until lightly browned; take care not to let them burn. Remove with a slotted spoon; drain on paper towel.

To serve, ladle Gazpacho into 6 individual serving bowls. Garnish each serving with some reserved cucumber, 3 grapes, 1 teaspoon sliced almonds, some garlic chips, and herbs.

Makes 6 servings.

COLONEL MUSTARD'S GRILLED PORK CHOPS

BARBARA MORGAN, Concord, CA

The spunky Dijon/garlic combo promise to make these tender chops a household favorite.

PORK CHOPS:
3 tablespoons whole mustard seeds
1 tablespoon coarsely ground pepper
1 tablespoon coarse salt
2 teaspoons dry mustard
6 boneless pork chops, 3/4-inch thick

BASTING SAUCE:
2 tablespoons Dijon mustard
4 cloves fresh garlic, peeled and crushed
1/2 cup dry white wine

GARLIC-MUSTARD SAUCE:
2 shallots, finely chopped
1 1/2 teaspoons dried tarragon
8 cloves fresh garlic, peeled and crushed
1/2 cup tarragon vinegar
1/4 cup brandy
4 egg yolks
1 tablespoon fresh lemon juice
1 tablespoon Dijon mustard
1 teaspoon stone ground mustard
Pinch cayenne pepper
1/2 cup plus 2 tablespoons unsalted butter, melted and hot
Salt
Coarsely ground pepper

To make rub for chops, coarsely grind mustard seeds and remaining spices with a mortar and pestle. Generously rub both sides of chops with the mixture. Let stand for 30 minutes.

Meanwhile, to make the Basting Sauce, whisk together Dijon mustard, garlic, and white wine; reserve.

To make Garlic-Mustard Sauce, cook shallots, tarragon, garlic, vinegar, and brandy over medium-high heat until almost all the liquid evaporates; reserve. In a blender, blend egg yolks, lemon juice, mustards, and cayenne for 10 seconds. With the blender running, pour in hot butter in a stream; process until mixture thickens. Add the shallot mixture; blend. Season with salt and pepper to taste; keep warm.

To serve, grill or broil the chops about 5 inches from heat source, turning several times, until cooked through, 12 to 15 minutes; baste frequently with Basting Sauce. Arrange chops on platter; top each with mustard sauce.

Makes 6 servings.

159

GARLIC SPRING ROLLS WITH GARLICKY-LIME SAUCE

KIM LANDHUIS, Fort Dodge, IA

The traditional Chinese egg roll sparkles anew with the pungent power of garlic and the plucky pucker of lime.

35	cloves fresh garlic, peeled, divided
2/3	cup fresh lime juice
1/2	cup fish sauce (nuoc man)*
1/4	cup bottled diced Jalapeños
2	teaspoons sugar
1/2	cup chopped water chestnuts
2	cups ground pork
5	green onions, chopped
1/2	cup grated carrot
2	teaspoons sugar
1	teaspoon salt
1	teaspoon coarsely ground black pepper
4	cups thinly sliced Napa cabbage (Chinese cabbage)
18	spring roll wrappers (thawed, if frozen)*
1/3	cup canola oil, or as needed
	Boston lettuce for garnish (optional)
	Pickled carrot for garnish (optional)
	Green onion brushes for garnish (optional)

sold in Asian grocery stores

To make sauce, in a food processor, finely chop 20 cloves garlic. Mix garlic with lime juice, fish sauce, lime juice, and sugar; reserve.

To make spring rolls, in a food processor, chop remaining garlic. In a bowl, thoroughly mix garlic with water chestnuts and next 6 ingredients. Gently fold in Napa cabbage.

On a work surface lightly dusted with cornstarch, wet the edge of 1 wrapper; put 2 tablespoons filling in the center. Fold 1 corner over filling. Fold in sides; roll tightly. Repeat with remaining wrappers. Heat half the oil (or more as needed) in a large non-stick frying pan; fry 9 rolls, turning frequently, until golden brown. Drain on paper towels; keep warm. Repeat with remaining rolls.

Arrange spring rolls on a serving platter with a bowl of sauce in the middle. Garnish with lettuce, carrot, and green onion.

Makes 6 servings.

160

SOFT GARLIC TORTILLA WRAPS WITH SPICY BARBECUE SALMON

BOB ANDRUSZKIEWICS, Watertown, MA

This is a delightfully festive dish for outdoor summer entertaining.

1½ lb. fresh fillet of salmon

1½ cups ketchup

½ cup Vietnamese chili-garlic sauce

8 large cloves fresh garlic, peeled and thinly sliced lengthwise

1 teaspoon salt

¼ cup extra virgin olive oil

12 corn or wheat tortillas

1 to 2 tablespoons warm water

2 cups chopped, fresh cilantro
  Juice of 1 lime

1 small head green cabbage, finely shredded

½ cup thinly sliced green onion

1 lime, sliced for garnish

1 red bell pepper, sliced for garnish

Cut fillet of salmon in half; reserve in a shallow baking dish.

To make barbecue sauce, mix ketchup, chili-garlic sauce, and one fourth of the garlic slices; pour 1 cup sauce over salmon. Reserve remainder to serve at the table. Make a paste with remaining garlic and salt; stir in olive oil. Reserve. Cook salmon skin-side down over high heat on a covered charcoal or gas grill for 7 minutes.

Place a damp tea towel in a hot cast-iron skillet; cover. Heat 1 tortilla at a time on a stove-top griddle or in a heavy frying pan. Brush each side with reserved garlic-oil mixture; generously sprinkle each side with cilantro. Keep warm and covered in the towel-lined skillet. Repeat with remaining tortillas. Reserve in skillet, covered tightly. When salmon has cooked 7 minutes, slide a wide, metal spatula between skin and flesh; flip salmon over back onto the skin.

Cover the grill; cook until salmon is firm to the touch, about 6 minutes. While salmon finishes cooking, mix remaining garlic-oil mixture with lime juice. Fold in cabbage and green onion. Garnish salad with lime slices and red bell pepper.

Serve salmon with cabbage salad and garlic tortillas. Each diner wraps chunks of salmon and cabbage salad in a garlic tortilla and dips it in reserved barbecue sauce.

Makes 6 servings.

161

BAKED STUFFED PORTABELLA MUSHROOM CAPS

MARGARET ANN BAVARO, Colts Neck, NJ

This wonderfully aromatic hors d'oevre is fun to assemble and well worth the effort.

DRESSING:
1/4 cup Balsamic vinegar
1 clove fresh garlic, finely chopped
1 teaspoon garlic powder
1 teaspoon dried oregano
1/2 teaspoon salt
1/4 teaspoon freshly ground pepper
1/2 cup olive oil

MUSHROOMS:
1 head fresh garlic plus 6 cloves fresh garlic, finely chopped, divided
6 tablespoons olive oil, divided
1/3 cup shredded, fresh basil, divided
6 medium Portabella mushroom caps (6 to 8 oz. each)
3/4 cup marinated sun-dried tomatoes
6 oil-cured black olives, pitted
1 teaspoon capers
1/3 cup ricotta cheese
1/2 lb. field greens

DRESSING:
Whisk together vinegar and next 5 ingredients; whisk in oil. Reserve.

MUSHROOMS:
Remove outer skin of the garlic, leaving head in tact; put in a small baking dish. Drizzle garlic with 1 tablespoon olive oil; bake at 450 degrees, covered, until soft, about 45 minutes. When garlic is cool enough to handle, squeeze garlic out of each clove; reserve. Sauté the remaining chopped garlic and 3 tablespoons basil in 3 tablespoons olive oil until garlic is aromatic, about 3 minutes; reserve. Put the mushroom caps gill-side down on a greased 11" x 17" baking sheet. Horizontally cut a slice off the top of each mushroom; reserve tops. In a food processor puree tomatoes with 2 tablespoons olive oil. Add remaining basil, olives, and capers; puree. Spread one sixth of tomato mixture inside each mushroom; reserve. Mix reserved roasted garlic and ricotta cheese; spread 1 heaping tablespoon over tomato mixture in each mushroom. Replace reserved mushroom caps. Drizzle reserved garlic-basil mixture over mushroom tops. Bake at 400 degrees until mushrooms are just tender, about 8 minutes. Divide field greens among 6 serving plates; top each with a mushroom. Drizzle 2 tablespoons reserved dressing over each plate.

Makes 6 servings.